THE PHILOSOPHY OF RELATIONS

BIBLIOTHECA INDO-BUDDHICA NO.—66

सम्बन्धपरीक्षा

THE PHILOSOPHY OF RELATIONS

(Containing the Sanskrit Text and English Translation of Dharma Kīrti's Sambandha-parīkṣā with Prabhācandra's Commentary)

By

V.N. JHA.

M.A. (Sanskrit), M.A. (Comparative Philology,)
Ph. D., Kāvya-Vyākaraṇa-Veda-Tīrtha

SRI SATGURU PUBLICATIONS
A Division of
INDIAN BOOKS CENTRE
DELHI—INDIA

Published by :
SRI SATGURU PUBLICATIONS
a division of
INDIAN BOOKS CENTRE,
Indological and Oriental Publishers
40/5, Shakti Nagar,
Delhi—110007
INDIA

First Edition—Delhi 1990

ISBN—81-7030-208-0

Printed in India at :
Kiran Mudran Kendra,
A-38/2, Maya Puri, Phase-I,
New Delhi-110064.

गुरुर्ब्रह्मा गुरुर्विष्णुर्गुरुर्देवो महेश्वरः ।
गुरुः साक्षात् परं ब्रह्म तस्मै श्रीगुरवे नमः ॥

DEDICATED
TO
THE FEET OF

Paṇḍita Sītākānta Ācārya
who laid foundation of my academic life

Acknowledgements

No word can express my feeling of indebtedness to my *paramārādhya guru*, Paṇḍita T.S. Śrīnivāsa Śāstrī under whose feet I studied the *Sambandha--parīkṣā* of Ācārya Dharmakīrti along with the Commentary of Prabhācandra.

My career of Sanskrit learning began at Raiganj (Dist. West Dinajpur, West Bengal), my home-town. It was 1956 when I came in contact with a great traditional Sanskrit Scholar, Paṇḍita Sītākānta Ācārya of Madhusūdana Catuṣpāṭhī, Raiganj. It was Paṇḍita Ācārya, the great scholar of *Mugdhabodha-vyākaraṇa* and an embodiment of poetic genius, who initiated me into traditional learning and encourged me with all his fatherly affections for deeper and higher Sanskrit learning. As a token of my deep sense of gratitude, therefore, I dedicate this volume to him.

My students have been my constant source of inspiration. It is only while teaching them Indian logic I developed keen interest in the problem of philosophical relations. The present volume is an exercise of that interest. I bless them all.

While preparing the Press copy, Dr. Ujjwala Panse, Dr. Nirmala Ambiye, Dr. Arun Ranjan Mishra, and Dr. Bhagyalata Pataskar, all my students and colleagues, have helped me. I am thankful to all of them.

Miss Sunita Nagpal, Mr. Valvi and Mrs. Bhalerao had typed the Press Copy. I am indebted to them.

I thank from the core of my heart Mr. Sunil Gupta, of Indian Books Centre, for bringing out this volume and I am indebted to his whole family for treating me with honour and affection. May The Almighty Lord Śiva bestow choicest blessings on the entire family !

V. N. Jha

Contents

Introduction

0.0 *THE PROBLEM*

The problem, in short, is whether there is a real entity called *Relation*. In other words, is there anything called Relation which is real ? 'No' is the answer of the idealists and 'yes' is the reply of the realists. By 'idealists' I mean the Buddhists and the Advaitins and by 'realists' I identify the Nyāya-Vaiśeṣikas, the Mīmāṁsakas and the other pluralists.

In fact, by 'idealism' we are to understand a view according to which I, we, you, he, they, table, chair—in other words, the entire world of our experience is our mental creation and so if our experience reveals any thing as a Relation, it has to be an illusion. To be nearer their stand, our experience prompts our behaviour: that experience reveals a number of things in a connected form : since these connections are our mental constructs, they are falsely projected outside; hence our behaviour is also illusory.

To understand it in the language of Nyāya-Vaiśeṣika, our behaviour depends upon a determinate cognition (*savikalpaka-jñāna*) : a determinate cognition reveals a structure of qualifier-qualificand type; such a structure is not possible without the involvement of an entity called Relation between the qualifier and the qualificand. But since, in reality, it is the mind which connects things encoded in language, the idealists have taken the relation to be an imaginary entity. As against this, the realists hold that since there is no reason why one should consider a determinate cognition as a false cognition, there is no reason to say that the Relations involved in the structure of a determinate cognition are false.

To this the idealists may advance an argument that the things appearing existent outside are projections of the mind and hence when the things themselves are not real where does the question of the reality of the relations arise ? The nihilists establish the falsity of the external world by saying that since a single thing possesses single form (*ākāra*) and since such a form appears in the cognition of that thing, the fact remains that the thing is in the mind and what appears outside is merely the projection of the mind. Thus, the external world is merely a mental creation and as such does not have any reality what-so-ever.

The realists' solution to this problem is very simple. They say that they can explain the presence of a thing in the knowledge by accepting a Relation called *Viṣaya-viṣayibhāva* 'Container-and-contained relation'. Through this relation any object can appear in the knowledge and hence there is no necessity to deny the existence of an outside world. Nevertheless, one entity will retain only one form. Therefore, there is no reason for the denial of the reality of the external world.

The idealists may raise further doubt by saying that the answer given by the realists involves the fault of endless regression. That is, the reality of a relation has to depend on the reality of the relation of *viṣaya-viṣayi-bhāva.* The reality of the relation of *viṣaya-viṣayi-bhāva* has to depend upon another knowledge which will require the *viṣaya-viṣayi-bhāva* relation. And in this way there will be no end to postulate such knowledge and hence the endless regression.

But this defect can be removed by the realists by saying that *viṣya-viṣayi-bhāva* relation is not a distinct entity; it is a self-linking relation (*svarūpa-sambandha*). In that case, the very knowledge of object will reveal that relationship of *viṣaya-viṣayi-bhāva* also, because this relation is either of the form of knowledge or of the form of object and in the *anuvyavasāya* both can appear.

Thus, since the relationship of *viṣaya-viṣayi-bhvāa* can be ascertained, the relationships like 'contact', 'inherence', etc. can also be ascertained to be true. Hence, a relation is a reality. This is what a realist will prefer to argue.

The acceptance of the reality of the *viṣaya-viṣayi-bhāva* relationship also establishes the external existence of things which we know and with which we behave throughout our life. Thus, since a determinate knowledge can be true, its objects namely, the qualifier, qualificand and the relation relating the qualifier to the qualificand can also be true.

Moreover, since our entire consistent behaviour depends upon a true determinate cognition, any relation involved in such a true cognition has to be true and hence a reality.

1.0 *WHAT IS A RELATION?*

The next question which will be in order is : What is the nature of a relation ? In other words, what can be the characteristic definition of a relation ?

The obvious answer will be : since a relation connects one with the other, the basic characteristics of a relation is that it rests on two entities (*dvisṭhaḥ sambandhaḥ*).

Thus when one hand is connected with the other, the relation (contact) rests on both the hands; when a blue colour is seen in a cloth, the relation (inherence) rests on both the blue colour and the cloth; when we see a wheel moving, the relation (inherence) exists on both, the movement and the wheel; when a cloth is produced out of a bundle of threads, the relation (inherence) subsists in both the cloth and the threads; when it is observed that many individuals form one class, the relation (inherence) exists in both the class and the individuals.

All these cases suggest that a relation subsists in two things.

Thus, the following is the nature of a Relation (R) :

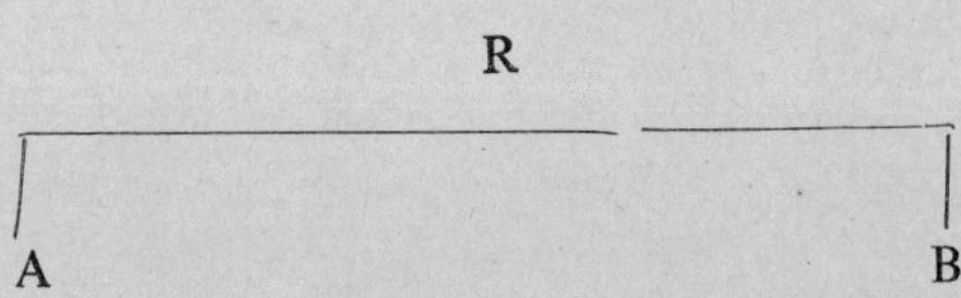

2.0 *VARIOUS PARAMETERS OF RELATIONS*

It is well-known a fact that the Navya—Naiyāyikas establish the reality of this universe through a structural analysis of cognitions.[1] This structural analysis involves various relations. Thus the Naiyāyikas have postulated various types of relations for this purpose for which sometimes they have been rediculed. There is a sarcastic verse in popular circulation in West Bengal,[2] most probably uttered by an Advaitin who finds no truth in any relation from the point of view of Ultimate Reality. Here, in this verse, a Naiyāyika has been addressed as *sambandhin* which will, although, mean in Sanskrit 'possessing relation', in Bengali, however, it means 'wife's brother' which is a slang.

The joke apart, the Navya-Naiyāyikas classified relations by using various parameters. Accordingly, the relation can be classified either as direct (*sākṣāt*) or indirect (*paramparā*).[3] By using another parameter some relations can be classified either as locus-pervading (*vyāpya-vṛtti*) or as non-locus pervading (*avypyavṛitti*).[4] Still another parameter if applied, the same relations can be again classified as either occurrence-exacting (*vṛttiniyāmaka*), or as non-occurrence-exacting (*vṛtti-aniyāmaka*).[5] Thus, as per the first parameter, contact (*saṁyoga*), inherence (*samavāya*) and *svarūpa* are called direct relations whereas co-locus-ness (*sāmānādhikaraṇya*) will be an indirect relation. As per the second parameter contact is a non-locus pervading relation, whereas inherence, *svarūpa* and co-locus-ness are locus-pervading relations.[6] Similarly, according to the third parameters, while contact, inherence and *svarūpa* are occurrence-exacting relations, the relation of co-locus-ness is a non-occurrence-exacting relation[7]. To this list of non-occurrence-exacting relations, can be added the relation of describerness (*nirūpakatva*) and described-ness (*nirūpyatva*)[8]. It should be further noted that some occurrence-exacting relation can act as non-occurrence exacting relation under certain situation. Such relation is the relation of contact. An occurrence-exacting relation is the relation which presents the content of a cognition or rather the qualifier and the qualificand, in the *ādhārādheya*--form. Thus, when the cognition arises in the form : There is a pot on the ground; the contact between the pot and the ground will be occurrence-exacting. Similarly, when the cognition arises that 'the left hand is on the right hand by contact, the contact is considered to be the occurrence-exacting relation. But if the cognition arises that 'the left hand is connected with the right hand when both the hands are horizontally placed side by side, the same contact will be considered as a 'non-occurrence-exacting' relation[9]. Inherence, is a permanent relation and so there is no chance of re-arranging its relata and hence it is always an occurrence-exacting relation. So far the *svarūpa*-relation is concerned, it can be either an occurrence-exacting relation or non-occurrence-exacting relation.

2.1 *OCCURENCE—EXACTING RELATIONS*

The Navya Naiyāyikas use the term *pratiyogin* normally in three situations :

(1) In the situation of an absence,

(2) In the situation of similarity, and
(3) In the situation of a relation

To illustrate, when we say *bhūtale ghaṭo nāsti*, 'there is no pot on the ground' or to be precise when we say *bhūtale ghaṭābhāvaḥ asti*, 'there is absence of pot on the ground', the pot is said to be the *pratiyogin* or counterpositive of the absence of pot and the ground is said to be the *anuyogin*.

[*ghaṭa*]← ——————→[*abhāva*]
(*pratiyogin*) |
[*bhūtala*]
(*anuyogin*)

Thus, absence has a *pratiyogin* and an *anuyogin*.

Similarly, when we say that *candra iva mukham* 'the face is like the moon', or to be precise, when we say *candra-nirūpita-sādṛśyavat mukham*, 'the face possesses the similarity described in terms of the moon,' the Navya Naiyāyikas call the moon as the *pratiyogin* of the similarity and the face or the locus of similarity as the *anuyogin*.

[*candra*]← ——————→[*sādṛśya*]
(*pratiyogin*) |
[*mukha*]
(*anuyogin*)

Thus, similarity has a *pratiyogin* and an *anuyogin*.

Likewise, when we say *ghataḥ bhūtalena saṁyuktaḥ*, 'the pot is connected with the ground' or to be precise, when we say, *ghaṭasya saṁyogaḥ bhūtale asti* 'the ground possesses the contact of the pot', the pot is said to be the *pratiyogin* of the contact and the ground is said to be the *anuyogin*.

[*ghaṭa*] (*pratiyogin*)
|
| ←(*saṁyoga*)
|
[*bhūtala*] (*anuyogin*)

Thus, a relation has a *pratiyogin* and an *anuyogin*.

In this section, however, I want to discuss the first situation only, namely, that of an absense. Absense has a *pratiyogin*. What does it mean ? It means that what obstructs the knowledge of an absense is the *pratiyogin* of that absence. The presence of *ghaṭa* obstructs the knowledge of the absence of *ghaṭa* and so *ghaṭa* is said to be the *pratiyogin* of the absence of pot. A *pratiyogin* of an absence is, as it were, the *virodhin* of the knowledge of its absence.

Once it is accepted that *ghaṭa* in the absence of *ghaṭa* is a *pratiyogin*, we must accept that there comes to reside a property called *pratiyogitva* or *pratiyogitā* (counterpositiveness) in *ghaṭa*. To be more precise, *ghaṭa* becomes the locus of *pratiyogitā*.

When someone says that *bhūtale ghaṭo nāsti* the following questions arise in our mind :

(1) Whether the locus of the counterpositiveness is any one individual pot, or,

(2) all pots

(3) Whether the counterpositiveness exists only in the pots and not in anything other than pot, namely in cloth etc.

(4) Whether this absence of pot is with regard to the absence of pot in the *kapālas* (two halves) i.e. in the parts.

(5) Or it is the denial of the relation of the pot with the ground.

The Navya Naiyāyikas try to answer these questions by the help of the concept of *avacchedaka*. Thus, whether the locus of a counterpositiveness is one pot or all pots can be made clear by introducing the delimitor of that counterpositiveness. In other words, if it is shown that the del mitor of that counterpositiveness is *tadghaṭatva* it will be clear that the counterpositiveness exists only in that particular *ghaṭa* and so it is an absence of only one pot. But if the delimitor is simply *ghaṭatva* it implies that it is an absence of all pots and the counterpositiveness exists in all pots because its delimitor exists in all pots.

It can be further observed that one can say *tatra nīlaghaṭo nāsti* even if blue, red and white pots exist there. But one cannot say *tatra ghaṭo nāsti* in the same situation. This clearly demonstrates that since in the first case the delimitor of the counterpositiveness is *nilaghaṭatva* one could say *nilaghaṭo nāsti* and since in the second case it is simply *ghaṭatva* that delimits the counter-positiveness, one could not say *ghaṭo nāstt*. In other words, the presence of the *pratiyogin* or *virodhin* obstructed the knowledge of the absence.

On this ground the Navya Naiyāyikas made the following generalisation :

pratiyogitā - avacchedaka-avacchinna - adhikaraṇatayā sākam abhāvasya virodhaḥ.

An absence is contradicted by the *adhikaraṇatā* of that which possesses the delimitor of the counterpositiveness of that absence.

Thus, the delimitor of the counterpositiveness decides whether a particulnr absence is of an individual or of all individuals of that class. By this we have replied to questions (1) and (2).

The same concept of delimitor of a counterpositiveness also replies to question (3) because once it is known that *ghaṭatva* is the delimitor of the counterpositiveness, the locus of the counterpositiveness cannot be anything but the pots because a delimitor and that which is delimited by that delimitor must have one and the same locus,

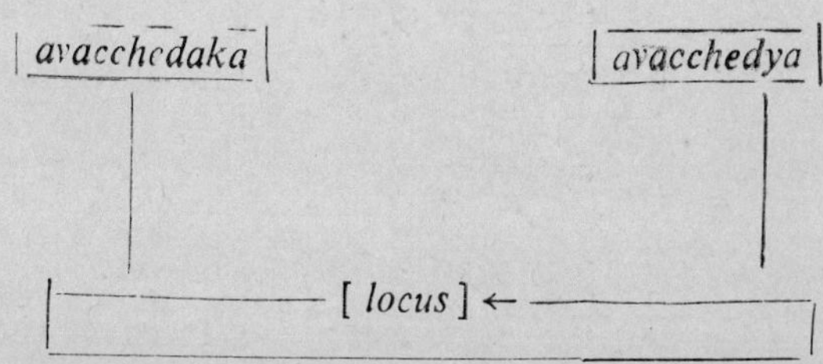

Thus, the locus of the counterpositiveness of the absence of pot must be pot only and cannot be anything other than pot.

As regards the questions (4) and (5) the Navya Naiyāyikas have utilised the concepts of a relational delimitorness. Here, such a delimitor will be a relation. Whether an absence of pot refers to the absence of pot on the ground or in the *kapālas* can be made clear by introducing a relation that delimits the *pratiyogitā*. The relation by which the counterpositive exists somewhere is called the delimiting relation of the *pratiyogitā*. Thus, if the *pratiyogitā* of the absence of pot is delimited by inherence, it is clear that we are talking about the absence of pot in its parts because only in its parts the pot can exist by the relation of inherence. Similarly, if the relation which delimits the counterpositiveness of the absence of pot is contact it is obvious that it is the case of an absence of pot on ground or the like since the pot can exist on the ground by contact only.

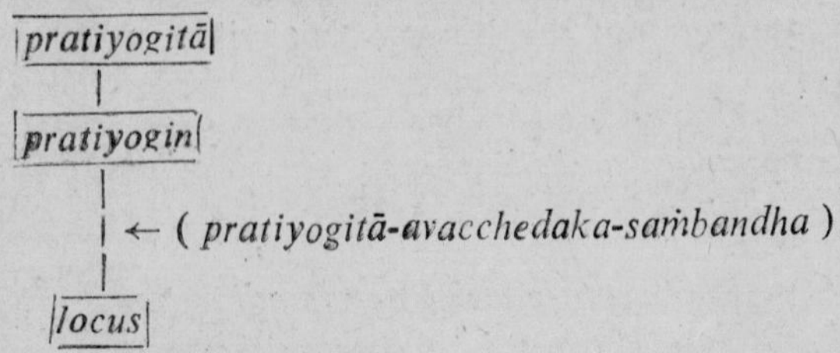

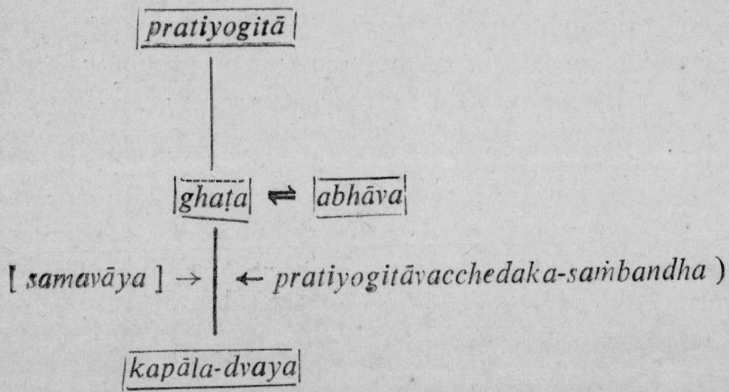

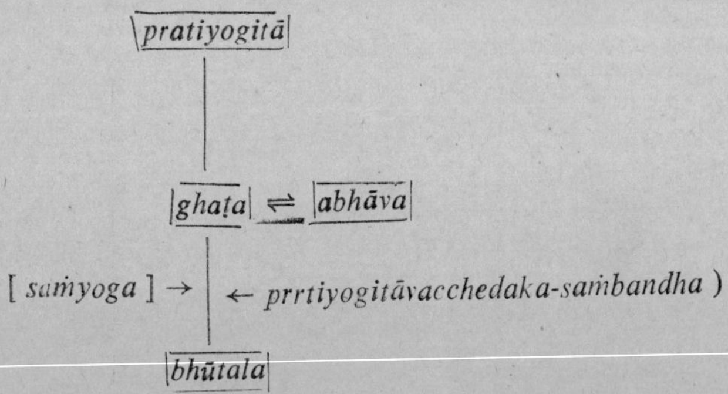

Thus, by introducing the concept of a delimiting relation the Neo-logicians have answered the questions (4) and (5).

In short, by introducing a delimiting property and a delimiting relation of the counterpositiveness the Neo-logicians have tried to make the following statement specific and unambiguous : *bhūtale ghaṭo nāsti.*

One cannot argue that the mention of *bhūtale* in the statement itself can make the expression unambiguous and specific since the pot can exist on the ground by the *kālika-sambandha* also. Thus, it is necessary to indicate the delimiting relation.

Now, by definition a delimiting relation of a counterpositiveness is that relation by which the counterpositive *exists* somewhere. In other words, the relation that generates the notion of *ādhārādheya-bhāva* can be a delimiting relation. For this reason I think, the Navyas say that the delimiting relation of a counterpositiveness has to be an occurrence-exacting relation, (*vṛttiniyāmaka-sambandha*). But does it imply that this dictum is to be universally applied ? If so, then it will pose a problem. We can use negation only where one can have the knowledge of *ādhārādheyabhāva* and not in any other case where such a notion does not arise. Thus, although we can say the following :

bhūtale ghaṭo nāsti

'There is no pot on the ground'.

tantuṣu paṭo nāsti

'There is no cloth in the threads'.

śaśe śṛṅgaṁ nāsti

'There is no horn on the hare'.

khe puṣpam nāsti

'There is no flower in the sky'.

ghaṭe viṣayatā nāsti

'There is no *viṣayatā* in the pot'.

bhūtale ghaṭābhvāaḥ nāsti

'There is no absence of pot on the ground'.

We cannot say the following :

Caitrasya dhanaṁ nāsti

'Caitra does not have wealth'.

Because there is no notion of *ādhārādheyabhāva* either between Caitra and *dhana* or between the meaning of the genitive suffix and *dhana*, if *svāmitva* is the meaning of the genitive suffix. The relation that exists between *svāmitva* and *dhana* is *nirūpya-nirūpaka-bhāva* which is obviously not a *vṛttiniyāmaka* relation since nobody has notion that *svāmitva* exists in *dhana* by this relation. *Svāmitva* exists in *svāmin* and not in *dhana*. Therefore, if we mean that there is no *svamitva* in *dhana* by *nirūpya-nirūpaka-bhāva* relation, then this relation has to be accepted as the delimitor of the counterpositiveness of the absence of *svāmitva* in *dhana*. This will violate the dictum that occurrence-exacting relation alone can be the delimitor of a counterpositiveness.

In order to avoid this Raghunātha proposes that the meaning of the genitive suffix here should be *svatva* and not *svāmitva*. Now of course, the earlier difficulty is over because there is *ādhārādheya-bhāva* between *svatva* and *dhana* because *svatva* exists in the *sva*, namely, *dhana* by *svarūpa-saṁbandha* which is a *vṛttiniyāmaka-saṁbandha*.

But what about the case of mutual absence ? What is the relation there to delimit the counterpositiveness ? Let us examine the case of *ghaṭah paṭo na*. 'The pot is not cloth'. Here, the locus of the counterpositiveness can be either the pot or the cloth depending upon the intention of the speaker. But whatever may be the locus of the counterpositiveness, the delimiting relation of this counterpositiveness is the identity-relation because by this relation a pot exists in a pot and does not exist in cloth or a cloth exists in cloth but does not exist in pot.

Now the question arises : whether the identity relation is an occurrence-exacting relation or not.

Before we settle this problem let us, first, look at the actual definition of the mutual absence as put forward by the Navya-Naiyāyikas.

Navya Nyāya defines *anyonyābhāva* as *tādātmya-saṁbandha-avacchinna-pratiyogitāka-abhāvaḥ* i.e. an absence, the counterpositiveness of which is delimited by the relation of identity.

Now, if the earlier dictum that the delimiting relation of a counterpositiveness has to be an occurrence-exacting relation which is to be universally applied and if the delimiting relation of the counterpositiveness of a mutual absence is the identity-relation as it is so in the above definition, then automatically the identity relation has to be declared as an occurrence-exacting relation.

Let us examine one more case. While clarifying the statement of *siddhānta-vyāpti* of Gaṅgeśa, Raghunāthaśiromaṇi presents someone's view that the word *atyantābhāva* should be understood in the sense of *saṁsargābhāva* in the *siddhānta-vyāpti*, namely, ***pratiyogi-asamānādhikaraṇa - yatsamanādhikaraṇa - atyantābhāvāpratiyogita-vacchedakāvaccinnaṁ yan na bhavati tena samaṁ tasya sāmānādhi-karaṇyaṁ vyāptiḥ.***

Raghuṇātha points out that no purpose will be served by this interpretation. Not only that, it will invite narrow-application of the definition in a case where the *sādhya* is intended by the relation of identity. Let us analyse the following case :

Ayaṁ tādtāmyena gomān,
Gotva-vattvāt.

'This possesses cow by the relation of identity,
because it has cowness.

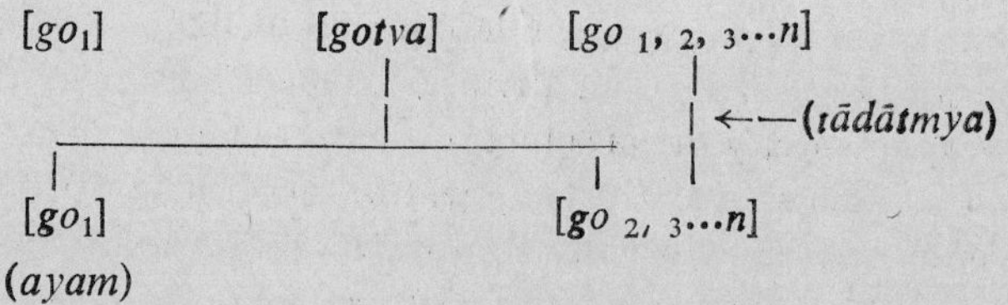

This is a true case of inference because wherever there is cowness there is cow by the relation of identity. But if in the Gaṅgeśa's definition of *vyāpti*, the word *atyantābhāva* is understood as *saṁsargābhāva*, the definition will not be applicable to the present case of inference because as per the requiremect the absence sharing the locus of *hetu* should be the absence whose counter-positiveness is delimited by the relation which delimits the *sādhyatā*. Here such a relation is the identity relation. And there is no *saṁsargābhāva* the counterpositiveness of which is delimited by the identity-relation. Hence, the narrow application of the definition of *vyāpti* in the abovementioned case.

The point that I want to make here is : can we talk of *tādātmya-sambandhāvacchinnapratiyogitā* at all ? Obviously this *pratiyogitā* cannot be the *saṁsargābhāvīyapratiyogitā* as is clearly denied above.

Then can this *pratiyogitā* be *anyonyābhāvīyapratiyogitā* ? The answer must be an emphatic 'yes' because we have already seen that mutual absence is defined as *tādātmyasambandhāvacchinnapratiyogitā-ka-abhāva.* If this is true then one must accept that *tādātmya* or identity-relation is the delimitor of the *anyonyābhāvīya-pratiyogitā.*

And if we want to maintain that the relation which delimits the counterpositiveness has to be an occurrence-exacting relation, then the identity-relation should also be treated as an occurrence-exacting relation.

But looking at the literature on Navya Nyāya I find that opinions are divided among the logicinas on this issue. While some want to treat it as a non-occurrence-exacting relation, others are not prepared to accept it to be so. That the opinions were divided on this issue is clearly reflected in Gadādhara's *Vyutpattivāda*.

Let us examine the consequences of both the stands. If identity relation is not treated as the occurrence-exacting relation then how to understand the expression *tādātmya-sambandhāvacchinna-pratiyogitā* in the definition of mutual absence will be a problem, since by corollary an occurrence-exacting relation alone can be the delimitor of the counterpositiveness of an absence. To get rid of this difficulty one will have to specify the meaning of the word absence as relational absence so that the above restriction will be applicable to relational absence only and not to mutual absence also as some Naiyāyikas have done Or if we do not want to narrow down the meaning of the word absence to 'relational absence' we should loosen the restriction to the effect that even non-occurrence-exacting relation can be the delimitor of the absential counterpositiveness and that such an attempt was already there is evident from the *Vyutpattivāda* of Gadādhara.

Or we can take the other stand that the identity-relation is also an occurrence-exacting relation in which case the universality of the restricting statement mentioned above is maintained. But can we take such stand ? Suppose, we do, what would be the consequences ? To my mind, the immediate consequence will be an objection that no one has such an experience that x possesses x by the relation of identity and since there is no such experience, there can be no such linguistic expression as *ghaṭaḥ ghaṭavān*.

As regards the question of non-experience of x on or in x by the relation of identity, one may argue that it is not a necessary condition that for each and every logical postulation there must be corroboration by direct experience. Because inspite of our non-experience as the logic demands that at least for a moment a substance is without quality and action, similarly, even if there is no direct experience one should acc ept on logical grounds that the identity-relation is an occurrence-exacting relation because it is conceived as the delimitor of the absential counterpositiveness.

With regard to the second point, one does find that the logicians use such sentences as follows :

tādātmyasambadhena ghaṭaḥ svasminn eva vartate

(*Kiraṇāvli* on the *Nyāyasiddhāntamuktāvalī*, p. 60).

Here the expression *vartate* clearly states that *ghaṭa* is in *ghaṭa* by the relation of indentity.

If someone argues that such expressions as quoted above are the expressions of analysis and not of the common observer, then we should try to understand the expression of *pratiyogitā* in the definition of the mutual absence. Now, if we understand the expression *pratiyogitā* as *sambandhitā* then although the above difficulty of identity, being the delimitor of the *pratiyogitā*, will be over, still it will create another problem namely, it will allow any non-occurrence exacting relation to be the delimitor of the *pratiyogitā*. Thus the statement that the delimiting relation of a counterpositiveness must be an occurrence exacting relation will not remain valid. Accordingly, the non-occurrence-exacting relation like *nirūpakatva* etc. will also become the delimitor of the counterpositiveness in the case of *na idaṁ caitrasya dhanam*.

And so *svāmitva* can be easily taken as the meaning of the genitive case-ending. But Raghunātha in his *Nañvāda* has clearly stated that if *svāmitva* is accepted as the meaning of the genitive case-ending here then, even if the wealth belongs to Caitra one can say *nedam Caitrasya*, which is absured. Gadādhara while interpreting this in his *Vyutpattivāda* further says that if *svāmitva* is accepted as the meaning of the genitive suffix then one cannot say that Caitra does not possess the wealth even if the wealth does belong to him since an absence whose counterpositiveness is delimited by the non-occurrence-exacting relation is not known to us. Moreover, if it is argued that in that situation the absence, whose counterpositiveness is delimited by *āśrayatā*-relation, will be understood then it will lead to the situation that even if the wealth actually belongs to Caitra one can say *nedam caitrasya*, because it is a fact that *svāmitva* does not exit in the wealth by the relation of *āśraya tā*.

This implies that we cannot allow the non-occurrence-exacting relation to be the delimitor of the counterpositiveness and thereby we cannot interpret the *pratiyogitā* in the sense of *sambandhitā* also.

But we find that later on Gadādhara argues in favour of a non-occurrence-exacting relation being the delimitor of an absential counterpositiveness in his *Vyutpattivāda*. He asks :

Vṛttyaniyāmakasambandhasya abhāvapratiyogitāvacchedakatve doṣaḥ kaḥ ?

To this the opponent points out that it will involve *gaurava*, to which Gadādhara says he does not care for such *gaurava*. He says :

astu etad gauravam. upadarśita-bahuvidha-lāghavena īdṛśa-gauravasya akiñcitkaratvāt.

Thus a non-occurrence-exacting relation can also be the delimitor of the absential counterpositiveness. Nevertheless the relations like *nirūpakatva* etc. remain non-occurrence-exacting relations.

In the background of these facts we can draw the following conclusions :

(I) Either we should delimit the scope of the generalisation that the delimitting relation of the counterpositiveness must be an occurrence-exacting relation saying that it is true only with reference to the counterpositiveness relating to the relational absence.

(II) Or we should allow a non-occurrence-exacting relation also to be the delimitor of the counterpositiveness as Gadādhara has preferred. But this does not solve the problem raised in connection with *nedam caitrasya dhanam*.

(III) So far as the identity relation is concerned, we should accept that it is an occurrence-exacting relation so that the said generalisation that only occurrence-exacting relation can be the delimitor of the absential counterpositiveness, remains intact.

Notes and References

1. See Matilal B.K., *The Navya Nyāya Doctrine of Negation, HOS*, Volume 46, p. 31.
2. *Bhāvābhāvād yadi nātiriktaḥ sambandhibhiḥ svīkriyate padārthaḥ Janyāvināśi pratiyogiśūnyam Śrīlakṣmaṇakṣauṇīpater yaśaḥ kim.*

3. *Sambandhaś ca dvividhaḥ sākṣāt-paramparābhedāt, Navya-Nyāyabhāṣā-pradīpaḥ* (*NNBh. P*) by Maheśa chandra Nyāyaratna, Sanskrit College, Calcutta, 1973, p. 10.
4. *Saṁyoga-Vibhāga-Śabdātma-viśeṣa-guṇānām pradeśāvṛttitvam, Praśastapādabhāṣya*, Gaekwad Oriental Series no. 154, Baroda, 1971, p. 112. See Kandalī on it, *pradeśavṛttayaḥ avyapyavṛttayaḥ*
5. *punaś ca sambandho dvividhaḥ vṛttiniyāmakaḥ, vṛttyaniyāmakaśca iti. NNBh.* p. 16.
6. Since all these exist in their loci everywhere.
7. *Paramparāsambandhaḥ prāyaśaḥ sarva eva vṛttyaniyāmakaḥ, NNBh. P*, p. 18.
8. *Nirūpitatvasambandhasya vṛttyaniyāmakatayā, Vyutpattivāda* of Gadādhara with Prakāśa, Varanasi, 1931, p. 135.
9. *Samasūtrapātena sthityor ubhayoḥ saṁyogo'pi na vṛttiniyāmakaḥ NNBhP*, p. 17.

3.0 TYPES OF RELATIONS IN NAVYA NYĀYA

3.1 *SAṀYOGA AND SAMAVĀYA*

Given such a concept of a relation, 'the contact' can be a relation, and so also 'the inherence'.

If this R is either 'contact' or 'inherence', R is treated in the *Nyāya-vaiśeṣika* system as a distinct entily different from A and B.

3.2 *SVARŪPA*

But it is not always the case that R is either 'contact' or inherence; it may be other type of relations too. For instance, the R can be a cause-and-effect relationship. Now the question arises : what is this cause-and-effect relationship ? The standard answer found in the house of the realists is, R, in this case, is not a distinct entity but merely the property of being either the cause or the effect', which is an already accepted property and not an extra entity called the relation of cause-and-effect. Thus, here—

R = the property of being a cause or
the property of being an effect.

Now, if this is the nature of R here, it exists either in the cause or in the effect but not in both and hence how does it satisfy the general characteristics of a relation ? This has been the standard objection of the idealists against accepting a relation of the type of cause-and-effect. Under this category of relations will come a huge number of relations like the following :

1.	*Pitṛ-putra-bhāva*	'father-son-relationship'
2.	*guru-śiṣya-bhāva*	'teacher-taught-relationship'
3.	*sādhya-sādhana-bhāva*	'accomplished-accomplisher-relationship'
4.	*vācyā-vācaka-bhāva*	'expressed-expresser-relationship'
5.	*nirūpya-nirūpaka-bhāva*	'described-describer-relationship'
6.	viṣaya-viṣayi-bhāva	'content-container-relationship'
7.	*vyāpya-vyāpaka-bhāva*	'pervaded-pervader-relationship'
8.	*avacchedya-avacchedaka-bhāva*	'delimited-delimitor-relationship'
9.	*pratibadhya-pratibandhaka-bhāva*	'obstructed-obstructer-relationship'
10.	*viśeṣya-viśeṣaṇa-bhāva*	'qualificand-qualifier-relationship'
11.	*viśeṣya-prakāra-bhāva*	'qualificand-qualifier relationship'
12.	*prakāra-prakāri-bhāva*	'qualificand-qualifier-relationship'
13.	*pratiyogi-anuyogi-bhāva*	'counterpositive-locus relationship'
14.	*ā lhāra-ādheya-bhāva*	'locus-located relationship'
15.	*āśraya-āśrayi-bhāva*	'locus-located relationship'
16.	*lakṣya-lakṣaṇa-bhāva*	'to be defined-and-definition-relationship'
17.	*kārya-kāaraṇa-bhāva*	'effect-and-cause relationship'
18.	*janya--janaka-bhāva*	'produced-and-producer-relationship'
19.	*pratipādya pratipādaka-bhāva*	'demonstrated-and domonstrator-relationship'
20.	*sambandhi-sambandha-bhāva*	'related-and-relation relationship'

and hundreds of similar relations.

These relations are called *svarūpa-sambandha* 'self-linking relation'. These are not distinct relations in the sense a 'contact' or an 'inherence' is a distnict relation, because contact and inherence are distinct *padārtha*. Here if we replace *bhāva* in all the twenty cases mentioned above by *-tā* we will get forty properties *marked* with *-tā* suffix as follows :

1. *pitṛtā*
2. *putratā*
3. *śiṣyatā*
4. *gurutā*
5. *sādhyatā*
6. *sādhanatā*
7. *vācyatā*
8. *vācakatā*
9. *nirūpyatā*
10. *nirūpakatā*
11. *viṣayatā*
12. *viṣayitā*
13. *vyāpyatā*
14. *vyāpakatā*
15. *avacchedyatā*
16. *avacchedakatā*
17. *pratibadhyatā*
18. *pratibandhakatā*
19. *viśeṣyatā*
20. *viśeṣaṇatā.*
21. *viśeṣyatā*
22. *prakāratā*
23. *prakāratā*
24. *prakāritā*
25. *pratiyogitā*
26. *anuyogitā*
27. *ādhāratā*
28. *ādheyatā*
29. *āśrayatā*
30. *aśrayitā*
31. *lakṣyatā*
32. *lakṣaṇatā*
33. *kāryatā*
34. *kāraṇatā*
35. *janyatā*
36. *janakatā*
37. *pratipādyatā*
38. *pratipādakatā*
39. *sambandhitā*
40. *sambandhatā*

These forty properties form twenty pairs and are treated as relations. These are treated as relations because unless we treat them as relation we cannot explain the determinate cognitions which they generate. Thus, unless we assume a relation between *pitṛ* and *putra*, they cannot be known and referred to by these terms. Before a man gets a child he is not called *pitṛ*, but he is *putra* of some *pitṛ*. Thus in him there is *putratā* which is described in terms of *pitṛtā* of his father. But when he gets a son, a new property called *pitṛtā* is produced in him which is discribed by the *putratā* of his son. Thus, these acquired properties themselves functions as relation between the pairs. These properties could not be included in the given seven categories of the Nyāya Vaiśeṣika and hence Raghunātha Śiromaṇi argues in his *Padārthatattvanirūpaṇa* for treating them as additional *pādārthas.*

But the question remains if these properties could be treated as relations how do they satisfy the general definition of a relation, namely, R, subsists in two things A and B ? Because if *putratā* is the relation or *pitṛtā* is the relation, it is in *putra* only or in *pitṛ* only. *Putratā* does not exist in *pitṛ* and *pitṛtā* does not exist in *putra* with the same terms of reference.

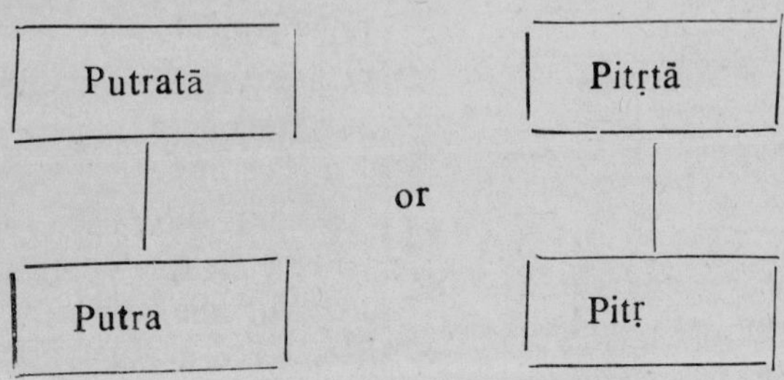

So, how *putratā* or *pitṛtā* be treated as a relation ?

The solution offered by the Navya Naiyāyikas to this problem is as follows :

They say that it is true that *pitṛtā* does not exist in *putra*, but it is not true that it does not exist there at all. The fact is this that any entity exists somewhere by some specific relation, and it is not correct to say that the entity should exist by one and the same relation everywhere. Thus, when *pitṛtā* exists in *pitṛ* directly by the relation of *āśrayatā*, it can exist in *putra* by the relation of *nirūpakatā*. Because, it is because of *putratā* in *putra*, the *pitṛtā* has come to reside in *pitṛ*. Thus, the *pitṛtā* in *pitṛ* is described in terms of *putra* and the *putratā* in *putra* is described in terms of *pitṛ*. Thus, although the direct locus of *pitṛtā* is *pitṛ*, *putra* can also be its locus since *putra*, describes the *pitṛtā* in *pitṛ*. Similarly, although *putratā* is directly located in *putra*; it can also claim *pitṛ* as its locus since it is because of *pitṛ*, he is called *putra*. Thus R at one end exists through *aśrayatā—sambandha* and at another end it exists through *nirūpakatā-sambandha*.

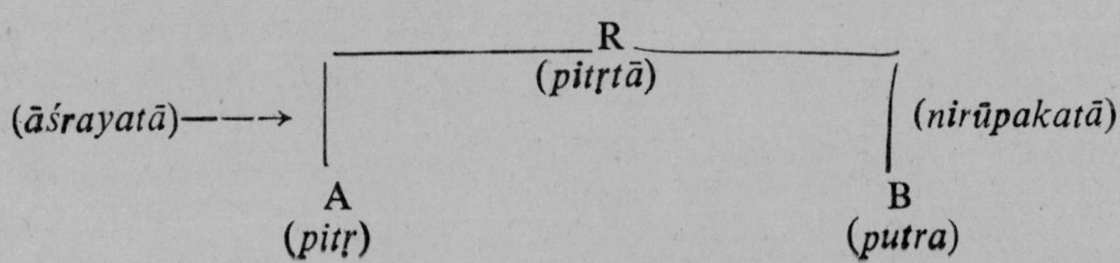

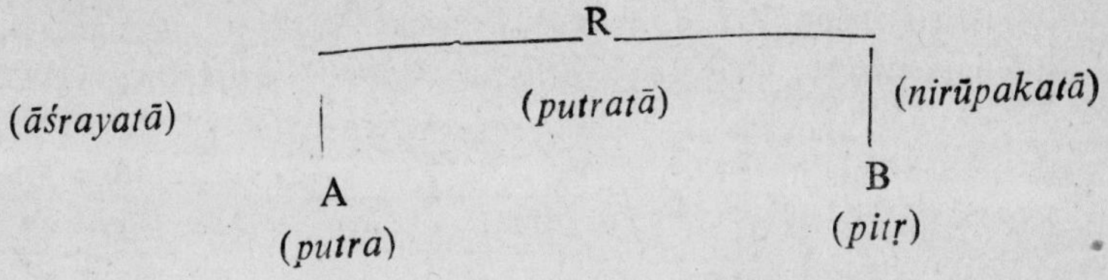

One may raise further objection by saying that what we find in the case of relations like contact or inherence that contact or inherence exists in its relata through one and the same relation and those relations are symmetrical relations, but here in the case of svarūpasambandhas there is no symmetry since one end of this relation is related through *aśrayatā* and the other through *nirūpakatā-sambandha.* In the case of contact both the ends are related through *śamavāya* and in the case of inherence both the ends are related through *svarūpa.*

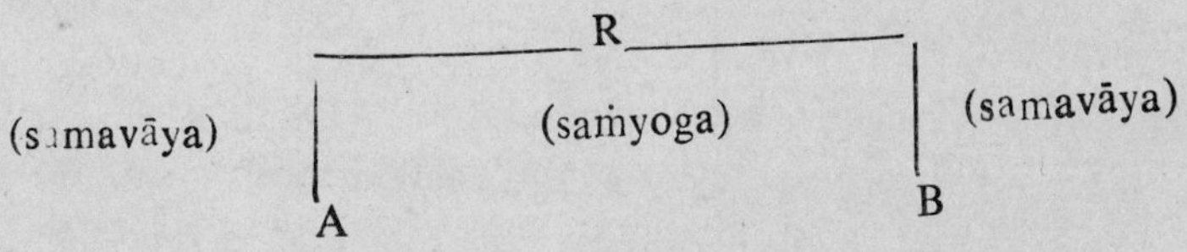

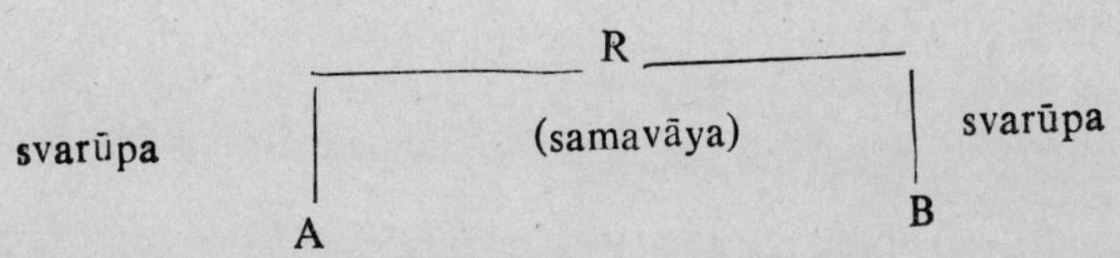

The Navya Naiyāyikas want that this symmetry need not be enforced in all cases. What is required is a relation, and not one and the same relation to relate R with A and B. If this is accepted then the problem is sloved and each property of the twenty pairs can be treated as a relation since they satisfy the general characteristic of a relation.

3.3 *PARYĀPTI*

There is a relation called *paryāpti-sambandha* in Navya Nyāya. It is accepted over and above the inherence-relation. It is a relation for explaining a cognition in which a *vyāsajya-vṛtti-padārtha* appears existing simultaneously in more than one locus. For instance, the number two is grasped as located simultaneously in two loci. Now, the fact that the number two is present in each and it is a quality is explained by accepting inherence and the fact that it is present simultaneously in both is explained by accepting an additional relation called *paryāpti*. This is also one type of *svarūpasambandha* only.

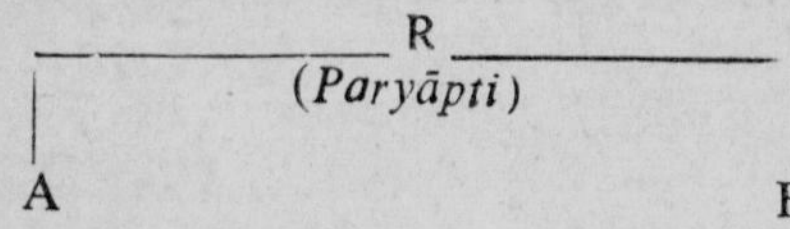

3 4 KĀLIKAVIŚEṢAṆATĀ OR TEMPORAL RELATION

Another relation is called *kālikasambandha* or *Kālikaviśeṣaṇatā-sambandha*. We can discuss it in detail since this has created a lot of confusion among scholars.

The Navya Naiyāyikas paraphrase *Svarūpa* as *viśeṣaṇatā*. This *viśeṣaṇatā* is further divided into two types : (1) *daiśika-viśeṣaṇatā* and (2) *Kālika-Viśeṣaṇatā*, while *daiśika-viśeṣaṇatā* can be further paraphrased as *deśanirūpita-Viśeṣaṇatā*, *kālika-viśeṣaṇatā* can be paraphrased as *Kālanirūpita-viśeṣaṇatā*. When the cognition arises that 'There is absence of pot on the ground' (*ghaṭābhāva-vat bhūtalam*) the absence of pot appears as the qualifier, the qualifierness of which is described by the qualificandness of the ground which is a place.[11] Similarly, when we cognise 'There is a pot in the universal time (*ghaṭavān mahākālaḥ*) pot appears as the qualifier, the qualifierness of which is described by the qualificandness of time.

Thus, temporal relation or *kālika-sambandha* is a *svarūpa sambandha* which is nothing but *kālika-viśeṣaṇatā*.

As we have already seen that *Svarūpa-sambandha* is not a distinct entity as such. The Navyas inform us that *svarūpa* is to be understood either as *ādhāra-svarūpa* or as *ādheya-svarūpa*. Thus, in the cognition 'There is absence of pot on the ground' there is nothing more than the absence of pot which is *ādheya* and the ground which is *ādhāra* simply because it is a qualified cognition (*viśiṣṭa jñāna*) which presents the content-structure of qualifier-qualificand type, we have to accept some relation between the qualifier and the qualificand, without which it is improper to call them as qualifier and qualificand and the knowledge as a qualified knowledge. Thus, in order to explain such cases, the Naiyāyikas have accepted something called *svarūpa--sambandha*.[21] Needless to say, that neither contact can be a possible relation between the absence of pot and the ground, because contact is possible between two substances only, nor inherence is possible there because that is possible only in the five positive cases like part and whole, quality and substance etc. etc. Time is conceived in Navya Nyāya Physics as a *nimitta-kāraṇa* to any effect since it is all pervading.[13] Whatever is produced is produced at a particular time. Time cannot be the material cause (*samavāyi-kāraṇa*) to all effects. Neither can it be a non-material cause of any effect because it is a substance and a substance can be only a material cause and never a non-material cause. At the same time, all effects are produced in time. Therefore, time is a *nimitta-kāraṇa* of all effects.[14] In other words, all effects are produced in time. Naturally, the question arises, what would be the relation by which the effectness present in all effects could be delimited ? Obviously, we cannot maintain either of the established relations namely, contact and inherence as the delimitor of the effectness. But without such a delimitor we cannot explain the reality of effects. Therefore, the Navyas advocate *Kālika-viśeṣaṇatā* as the delimiting relation of the effectness. Accordingly, they define time as :

Kālikasambandhāvacchinna-kāryatvāvachinna - kāryatā- nirūpita-tādātmyasambandhāvacchinna - adhikaraṇatvāvacchinna - kāraṇatāvattvaṁ kālatvam.[15]

This can be demonstrated diagrammatically as follows :

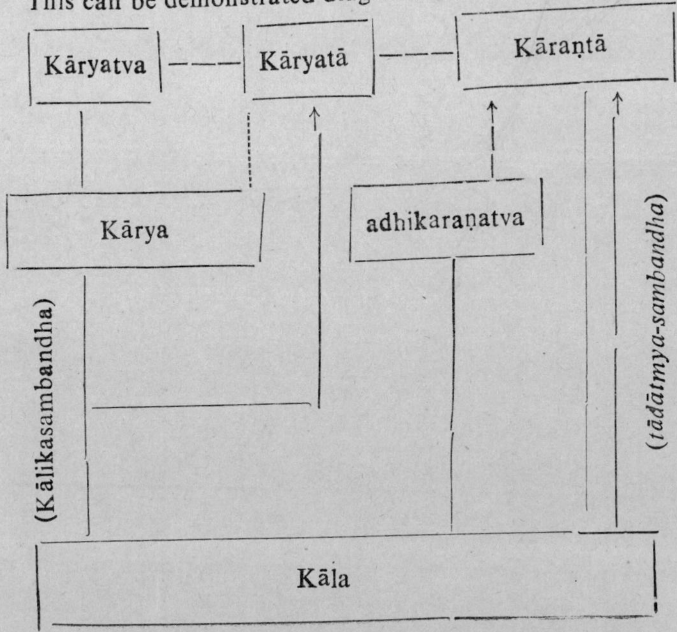

One may ask : What is the ground for accepting that for effect in general, time is a *nimittakāraṇa* ? The answer to this would be the following :

Tat-utpattyadhikaraṇasya—tadutpattihetutvam, tadutpattihetoś ca taddhetutvam iti niyama eva mānam[16] (If x is produced on y, y is the cause of the production of x and if y is the cause of the production of x, y is treated as the cause of x. This is the simple generalisation).

Again, if one asks that even if it is accepted that for a particular effect time has to be treated as the *nimittakāraṇa*, still what is the need of accepting time as the cause of effect in general ? This question can be answered on the basis of the following principle :

Yad-viśeṣayoḥ (kārya-kāraṇabhāvaḥ) tatsāmānyayoḥ api iti nyāyena kāryamātre kālasya hetutva-siddheḥ.[17]

If one asks a fundamental question: what is the proof that there is an entity called time ? the Naiyāyika would reply by the following inference :

Idānīm ghaṭaḥ ityākārakasūryaparispandaprakāraka – ghaṭa-viśeṣyaka—pratītiḥ—paramparā-sambandha— viṣayā, sākṣāt — sambandhābhāve sati viśiṣṭa—buddhitvāt.[18] The qualified cognition 'there is a pot in this moment of time' has the movement of the sun as its qualifier and pot as its qualificand, since there is no direct relation (between the movement of the sun and the pot) at the same time it is a qualified cognition'.

The indirect relation between the movement of the sun and the pot would be *svāśraya—saṁyogi—saṁyoga*[19] which can be represented as follows :

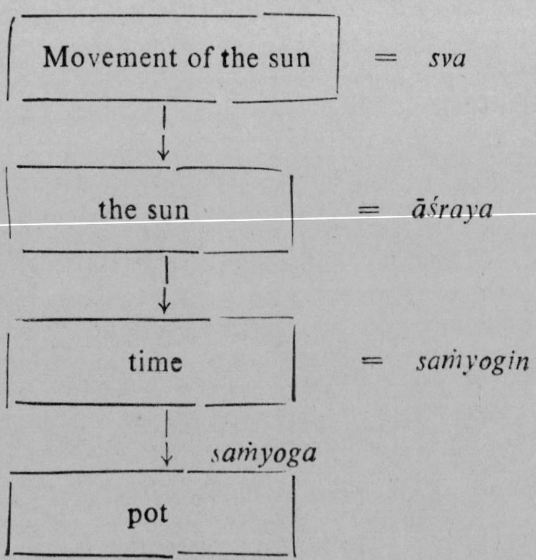

It can be observed that time is here established as a constituent of the indirect relation.

Further if one argues that let the sky be the *svāśraya-saṁyogin* sincesh sky is also all pervading, such an argument is not strong because there can be no decision in this regard because as the sky is all-pervading, so also the space (*diś*) and the soul (*ātman*). So why not *Itś* or *ātman* also should be treated as *svāśraya-saṁyogin* ? There is no conclusive argument for this. Moreover, we do say that the pot is in this moment of time. Hence, time alone appears as the constituent relation of the said indirect relation and not the sky or the space or the soul.[20]

This time is conceived as universal time (*mahākāla*) and as particular time (*khaṇḍakāla*). It is also said that any thing and everything exist in universal time (*jogatāṁ āśrayo maiaḥ or sarvādhārah kālaḥ*).[21]

Now when an entity directly exists in time the relation is the *sākṣātkālikaviśeśanatā*. By this direct relation all entities, whether produced or eternal exist in time and this relation can be considered as occurrence—exacting relation. In addition to this, we also find the use of another expression *kālika paramparā sambandha* by which one object is associated with another object. In other words, the object A is elated to the object B because both A and B share one and the same locus, remely, the time It can be presented as follows :

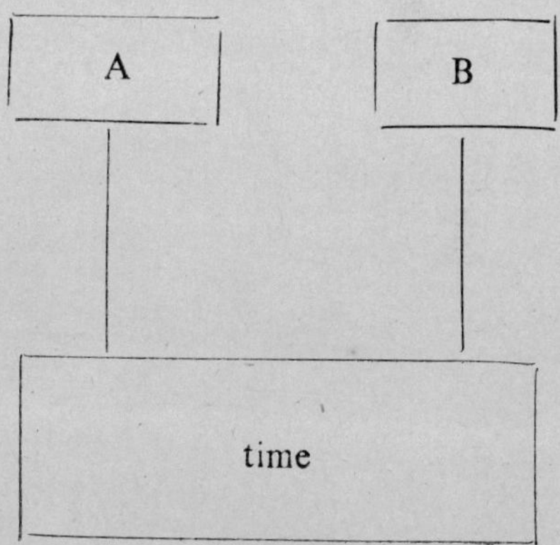

This is also called *kālikasāmānādhikaraṇya*. So far so good. But we meet with a difficulty of understanding when it is said that this *Kālikaparamparāsambandha* or *kālikasāmānādhikaraṇya* is an occurrence—exacting relation.[22] We are already aware of the notion of occurrence—exacting relation. So, how to understand the above statement ? In other words, how to understand that the object A is on or in B by the relation of *sāmānādhikaraṇya* which is an indirect relation ? There is no difficulty in understanding the statement such as A is related to B by the indirect relation of co-locusness; but it is difficult to conceive that A is in or on B by the same relation. This is the reason why H.H. Ingalls in his pioneering work *Materials for the study of Navya Nyāya* says :

"——It is quite inexplicable to me why the Naiyāyikas regard this relation as occurrence—exacting" (p. 79).

Following him, B.K. Matilal also opines that "It is really difficult to explain why a temporal *svarūpa* relation should be regarded as occurrence—exacting. The only explanation is that a time segment is regarded as a locus on par with a spatial locus" (see, *The Navya Nyāya Doctrine of Negation*, p. 49, fn. 16).

It appears to me that this problem can be solved if we strictly apply the Navya Nyāya notion of *Khaṇḍakāla* in such cases. In Navya Nyāya time segments are obtained by the concept of *upādhi*. The Navyas hold that since a particular object (say B) is produced at a particular time one can measure the segment of time with the help of this B. In other words, this B itself will represent the particular time segment. As long as B will be in existence it will represent that much duration of time,—(*Janyānāṁ kalopādhitvam*). Now when one says that A is on B by the temporal relation, it means that A is in the time delimited or segmented by B, as we say that there is the contact with monkey on a tree delimited by the branch of the tree. It can be put as follows :

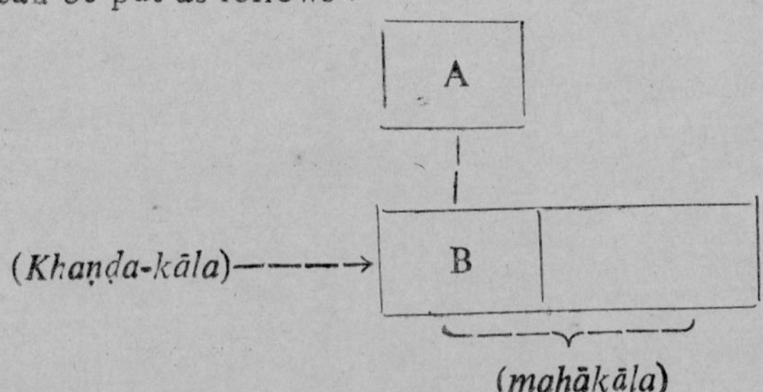

Thus, here, I think, there is no indirect temporal relation between A and B, but it is the direct temporal relation between A and B which causes the notion of *ādhārādheyabhāva* and hence *kālikasambandha* is an occurrence—exacting relation. If however, the notion is such that two things directly exist in time and they are mutually related, the relation will be an indirect one namely, *kālika-sāmānādhikaraṇya.* But in no case *kālikasāmānādhikaraṇya* will be an occurrence-exacting relation.

The above explanation will also be in consonance with the accepted theory of the *Navya Naiyayikas* that '*kale vṛttau deśaḥ avacchedakaḥ* and *deśe vṛttau kālaḥ avacchedakaḥ*. That is, when time is intended as the locus of an entity, the space becomes the delimitor of the occurrence of that entity. Similarly, when place is intended as the locus of an entity, the time will act as the delimitor of the occurrence of that entity. Thus, when one says '*asmin deśe asmin kāle ghaṭaḥ asti*', depending upon what is intended as the locus by the speaker, both time and space can be the delimitor in the alternative case.[23]

Thus, if the Navya Naiyāyika presents a paradox in the statement of *vyāpti* namely, *sādhyābhāvavadavṛttitvam*, saying that there is *ādheyatā* in the smoke in the lake by the temporal relation, one should not think that he is doing so by the indirect relation of *sāmānādhikaraṇya* but he is doing so by the direct temporal relation treating the lake itself as the *khaṇḍakāla* Otherwise, the *ādheyatā* in smoke described by the locus-ness of lake cannot be explained. Or else, we will have to admit. that the relation of co-locus-ness is an occurrence-exacting relation which is against our experience and hence absurd.

This in short is the notion of temporal relationship in NavyaNyāya.

Notes and References

10. *Tarkāmṛta* of Jagadīśa, Asaitic Society, Calcutta, 1974, p. 65.
11. *Viśeṣaṇatayā abhāvasya samavāyasya ca pratyakṣatvam*, *Tarkāmṛta* of Jagadīśa, Asiatic Society, Calcutta, 1974, p. 65.
12. On the basis of the following Inference :
    Ghaṭābhāva-vad bhūtalam ityākārakā—viśiṣṭabuddhiḥ viśeṣaṇa-viśeṣya—sambandha—viṣayā, viśiṣṭa—buddhitvāt, Kiraṇāvalī on ***Siddhānta—muktāvalī***, p. 57,

13. While commenting on the word *janakaḥ* (in *janyānām janakaḥ kālaḥ, verse 45 of the* Bhāṣāpariccheda), *Kiraṇāvalī* (p. 150) paraphrases *janakaḥ* as *nimittakāraṇam.*

14. *Kāryamātraṁ prati kālo na samavāyi—kāraṇam, dravyatvāc ca na asamavāyikāraṇaṁ kintu nimittakāraṇam eva iti bhāvaḥ, Kiraṇāvalī*, p. 150.

15. *Kiraṇāvalī*, p. 150.

16. *Ibid*, p. 150

17. *Ibid*, p. 151.

18. *Ibid*, p. 151.

19. *Ibid*, p. 151.

20. *Ibid*, p. 151.

21. *Bhāsapariccheada*, Verse no. 45.

22. *Mahakāla—khaṇḍakālayoḥ vṛttitāniyāmakaḥ kālika—viśeṣaṇatā-nāmakaḥ kaścit sākṣāt—sambandho' sti——*

23. Normally it can be observed that when two locative forms are used in a sentence, the meaning of one of them can act as the delimitor, for instance, when we say *vṛkṣe śākhāyāṁ kapisaṁyogaḥ asti*, 'There is the contact of the monkey on the branch on (=of) the tree', obviously, the branch of the tree acts here as the delimitor. Thus, the above sentence will mean *śākhāvacchinne vṛkse kapisaṁyogaḥ* 'There is the contact of the monkey on the tree delimited by the branch'. Similarly, either time or space can be the delimitor if both of them are found used in the locative case. It entirely depends on the intention of the speaker whether time or space will be the locus.

4.0 *ABOUT THE TEXT-SAMBANDHAPARĪKṢĀ*

I have taken the text of *Sambandhaparīksā* as it is printed in the *Dharmakīrti-nibandhāvalī* (2) edited by Swami Dwarakadas, *Bauddhabhāratī*, Varanasi, 1972. I am thankful to the editor for providing Sanskrit Paraphrases in the footnotes. This helps in grasping the text and this is why I too have taken the text along with the footnotes of Swamiji, with little changes here and there. I hope, he will be happy to see that this help has encouraged me to put the

Sanskrit text alongwith the commentary of Prabhācandra into English.

These verses of *sambandhaparīkṣā* occur in the *Prameya-kamalamārtaṇḍa* of Prabhācandra.

5.0 *CONTENT—ANALYSIS OF SAMBHANDHAPARĪKṢĀ*

(1) Sambandha (R)

dependency (*pāratantrya*) — close connection (*rūpaśleṣa*)

or

dependency

niṣpannayoḥ — *aniṣpannayoḥ* (śaśaviṣāṇavat)

If already *niṣpanna*, no question of any dependency

∴ dependency ≠ R (A)

(2) mixing or amulgamation

of two distinct things (a) — of two identical things (b)

If (a), then how mixing possible ?

If (b), then impossible, because relation must be between two distinct things.

∴ Mixing
or
amalagamation ≠ R (B)

rūpaśleṣa=*nairantarya*=*antarāla-abhāva*
abhāva=*tuccha*

∴ R ≠ reality (C)

More over

(3) *rupaśleṣa* (mixing or amalgamation)

total mixing (1) — by part only (2)

If (1), then the mixing of atoms
= one atom

If (2), then

(a) Part + *Paramāṇu* = *Paramāṇu* itself ?

Or, (b) Part + Paramāṇu = Part + Paramāṇu

If (a), then we cannot maintain that R is with a Part because Part is not left separately.

If (b), then again

(x) R_1 Part—t_1R2+*paramāṇu*=R_1 *Paramāṇu* ?

(y) R_1 Part_1 R2 Part_2 *Paramāṇu* ?

If (x) then again the same contigency like (a) above.

If (y) then *anavasthā* i.e.
repeating the same process again and again.

∴ *rūpaśleṣa* $\neq$ R (D)

Again,

(4) If x R y
then

R

different from (x) and (y) (a) — identical (b)

If (a), then how can we say : x and y are related ?

If (b), then either x or y or R exists and so there is nothing like x R y.

∴ R $\neq$ a reality (E)

Moreover,

(5) Or, let R be a thing, still

$$x \overset{r_1}{\text{———————}} R \overset{r_2}{\text{———————}} y$$

What will be r_1 and r_2 ?

The difficulties will be the same as above between x and y of R.

If r_1 and r_2 also are treated as reality, then again the same question will arise : What is the relation between r_1 and x and r_2 and y ? In this way it will lead to *anavasthā*.

$\therefore$ R $\neq$ reality (F)

(6) R = x, y

It is only imagination that connects x and y. And depending on this imagined relation the speaker uses the language by way of *anyāpoha* and thereby creating a *kāraka*-relation. In fact there is no relation of any *kāraka* with *verb* because everything is momentary. At the time of *kriyā*, *kāraka* is not there.

kalpanā——*kalpanāviṣaya*——*anyavyāvṛtta*——*śabdaviṣaya*

$\therefore$ R $\neq$ *kriyākārakasambandha* (G)

(7) Again Cause-and-Effect relation is also not possible because cause and effect do not exist together.

x——R——y
(Cause) (Effect)

How can R exist in x and y at a time ?

$\therefore$ R $\neq$ a reality (H)

(8) Nor can it be said that let this R exist in Cause and in Effect in a sequence and not at a time because when it exists in Cause it does not exist in Effect, so how can that R existing in Cause (= a single entity) be said to be a Relation ? It implies that R can exist without x or without y which is not the feature of a relation.

Nor can one say that R is a relation because x is expectant of R or y is expectant of R, because in that case R must produce some effect in x or y, but when R is in x, y does not exist, then how can R produce any effect in y, or vice versa ?

Even then if one says that R is a relation, then such a relation has to be accepted between the left horn and the right horn of an animal, which is absurd.

An R is that entity which exists in two things.

∴ *kāryakāraṇabhāva* $\neq$ R (I)

This also sets aside the possibility of inherence and contact as relations.

6.0. DHARMAKĪRTI *ON RELATIONS*

In the process of generation of a cognition Relation plays an important role. In realism it is an utter impossibility to acquire an expressible cognition without the ontological reality of a relation. An idealist on the other hand, can do away with a relation. Dharmakīrti who prepared a logical ground to argure in favour of idealism, going by the name of the philosophy of Yogācāra, wrote an independent treatise called *Sambandhaparīksā* in order to deny all relations proposed by a realist. In the present section an attempt is made to go into the reason which compelled Dharmakirti to do so.

Before analysing the arguments of Dharmakīrti it is necessary to recall the position of the realists like the Naiyāyikas with regard to the ontological status of a relation. Is relation a reality? Positive is the answer of the Naiyāyikas. Why should it be accepted at all? The Naiyāyikas start replying to this question by forwarding the following proof of Inference :

viśiṣṭabuddhiḥ viśeṣaṇa-viśeṣya-sambandha-viṣayā,
viśiṣṭabuddhitvāt,
daṇḍīpuruṣa iti viśiṣṭabuddhivat

Any knowledge which shows a qualifier-qualificand structure has three elements in it as its object, namely, the qualifier, the qualificand and a relation that connects the qualifier and the qualificand. The knowledge, namely, 'the man with a stick' has accordingly three things such as the stick, the man and the contact between the stick and the man.

There is also another logical assumption in the system of realism that the object of a true knowledge must be an ontological fact or reality. It is further assumed that such a real entity causes the cognition as its object in presence of the necessary conditions.

It is this assumption that does not allow the knowledge of sky-flower and conversely does not allow to posit an entity called sky-flower.

Thus from the above mentioned syllogism of the Naiyāyikas we are to accept a relation because without that we cannot explain a true and expressible cognition.

Naturally, if a cognition which is consistent with our behaviour is to be true we must accept a relation. This will be the stand of the realists.

Such a relation is of various types. A relation can be a contact occurring between two substances. Inherence is another relation accepted by the Naiyāyikas between quality and substance, action and substance, whole and its parts, generic character and the individuals and between particular (*viśesa*) and permanent substances. Where neither contact nor inherence can be accepted as a relation the Naiyāyikas, we have already seen, accepted a relation called *svarūpa* in order to explain a *viśiṣṭabuddhi*. This relation will vary from case to case depending upon the relata.

Again there are other types of relations. Let us consider the following sentences :

1. *tantuḥ paṭasya kāraṇam*
2. *daṇḍah ghaṭasya kāraṇam*

Here we are characterising *tantu* and *paṭa* and *daṇḍa* and *ghaṭa* in terms of cause and its effect which mutually describe each other. Unless there is a relation in the above mentioned cases neither thread can be said to be the cause of cloth nor cloth can be said to be the effect of thread. Similarly, the stick cannot be termed as cause and the pot cannot be termed as effect. Thus it is required to accept a relation called *kāryakāraṇabhāva*. Likewise the Naiyāyikas accept other relations such as *nirūpya-nirūpaka-bhāva* and the like as already demonstrated in section no. 3 above.

These are the relations which can be termed as direct relations. The Naiyāyikas also accept indirect relations such as *sāmānādhikaraṇya* (co-existenciality) and the like,

All these relations are ontological facts on which depend our true congnitions on which depend our consistent behaviour. This seems to be the realists stand-point.

Let us now see how Dharmakīrti looks at the relations. He says that if something is a relation it should be of any of the following types. In other words, if something is a relation it will have any of the following characteristics :

(1) Dependency is a relation.

(2) Amalgamation or contact is a relation.

(3) Expectancy is a relation.

(4) Cause--and—effect relationship is a relation.

(5) That which exists in two things is a relation.

But none of these natures of a relation is possible to be established and so there is no ontological reality of a relation.

If it is accepted that dependency is a relation one must prove that an object depends on it. But it is not a reality because in that case there are two alternatives.

(a) either the two relata say, x and y, have a relation, say, z after x and y have already accomplished their forms.

(b) or before that.

(a) is not possible because when x and y have already accomplished their forms there is no dependency as such.

(b) is obviously absurd because when x and y have not assumped their forms they do not exist and as such the question of existence of a relation between them does not arise.

Contanct also cannot be a relation because contanct with what ? If you say that one *paramāṇu* is connected with other *paramāṇu*, the next question can be put as follows :

Whether such a relation is total amalgamation of one with the other, or not. If you say yes. then two *paramāṇus* will form only one *paramāṇu*; and if the contact is with a part only then also we can ask the following;

Whether such a part is identical with the whole or not. If you say yes, it is not possible because no part will be left separately and thus contanct cannot be established as a relation. Naturally, you will have to treat parts and wholes as different. Then again, the same question will be put: whether the contact between the part and the whole is total or partial. If total, then again no part is left with which contact is possible. If partial then again the chain of questions will arise leading to *ad infinitum*. Therefore, contact cannot be a relation in reality.

Likewise expectancy also cannot be a relation. Because if *x* is said to expect *y*, two questions can be put :

Whether (a) being existent, *x* expects existent *y* or
(b) without being existent, *x* expects *y* ?

One cannot maintain the second alternative obviously because in that case two ficticious things also will have a relation which is naturally ficticious. The first alternative is also not possible because when *x* and *y* are already in existence it proves that *x* does not require *y*. Thus hardly there is relation called expectancy.

Similarly, there can be no relation called cause-and-effect. Because (1) a relation should exist in two things and it is not true with regard to this cause-and effect relationship because when that which is called as cause exists the other relatum called effect does not exist. (2) If it is said that cause and effect mutually describe each other and so such a relation exists in cause and effect in sequence, this is impossible because without requiring either effect or cause for its locus the relation of cause-and-effect is said to exist either in cause only or in effect only. And that which exist either in *kāraṇa* or *kārya* cannot be said to be a relation. (3) There is no chance of occurring of such relation in sequence, say, first in cause and then in effect because in that case it will mean that the cause is in need of an effect and cause requires that effect shoud necessarily produce something in cause. But such a help is difficult to be produced by effect because at the time of cause there is no effect. (4) If it is argued that since *x* and *y* are related to something *z*, *x* and *y* are called cause and effect respectively, it will lead to a very absurd situation. In that case, since say, number two is related to two things you should accept that one is the cause and the other is the effect—which is an absurdity. (5) If one argues that when it is observed that without something say, *x*, *y* does not come into existence, it is necessary to accept a relation called cause-and-effect. It is not necessary because even without accepting an entity called relation over and above *x* and *y* one can call *x* and *y* by the name of cause and effect on the basis of the presence and absence of *x*, causing presence and absence of *y*. What is the need of accepting an unreal relation ?

Nor can it argued that how x and y are called *kāraṇa* and *kārya* without accepting a relation between the two or in other words how different things which have individual names are called by the name of *kārya* and *kāraṇa*. It all depends on the speaker to give a particular name to thing in the way he looks at that particular thing. This does not establish a relation called *kāryakārṇabhāva*.

Since *kāryakāraṇabhāva* cannot be established as a relation over and above the relata, no relation of the types of inherence contanct etc., can also be established as real entities. The contact between the two threads is treated as non-material cause with reference to the effect namely, the cloth by the Naiyāyikas. Similarly, a whole is produced in its parts by the relation of inherence. Parts are the cause of the whole. In other words, there is cause and effect relationship between parts and whole. This is what the Naiyāyikas think. In this way the function of relation is shown by the realists. But none of these relations can be established as a reality because there is no reality of cause and effect relationship itself. Nor can we establish the reality of an expressible cognition in such situation.

Moreover, if x and y are called cause-and-effect respectively one can ask the following questions :

(1) Whether x and y are different from each other

or (2) x and y are identical.

(1) is not true because in that case x and y are settled with their own existence. (2) is also not true obviously.

If the Naiyāyikas argue that they call x and y as cause and effect respectively not because of the above ground but because there is a relation called cause and effect, it is also not tenable. Because the so called cause and effect relationship also requires another relation for its connection with both cause and effect. It amounts to saying that there is no direct relation called cause and effect in reality and so the cognition which reveals two things x and y as connected is an illusion.

Thus, if there is a direct relation between x and y that relation should connect x and y without any via-media but it is never the case. The Naiyāyikas say that x and y are connected with each other by the relation z only if z is related to both x and y by some other relation. Naturally, it is clear that z has no direct relation with x and y. Therefore, any cognition that reveals a direct connection between x and y has to be an illusion.

It is further argued by Dharmakirti that if it is said that since x and y are going to produce z and so x and y are called connected, it is absurd because how can they be called so before z comes into existence. Not only that if such a situation is accepted then any other factor responsible for z is also to be called connected, because it too produces z.

Over this the Naiyāyikas may clarify the position that it is not their intention. What they intend is that which maintains z is called connected and not all factors.

To this Dharmakirti says that what you call maintenance is not anything more than *anvayavyarireka*. There is nothing called *sthiti* (maintenance) as an entity. Thus a cognition that reveals a connection is not real and coversely a relation is not a reality. It is nothing more than an imagination.

From the above description two questions emerge : (1) why should Dharmakīrti be all out to deny a relation ? And (2) how could he succeed in doing so ?

The answer to the second question will help us know the motive of Dharmakīrti. He started with a premises that any expressible cognition has connection with name and form which are mental postulates and have no real external existence and since our all consistent behaviour is with such illusory objects, it is false. Thus, the cognition which can be expressed is false. Naturally, *viśiṣṭajñāna* is false. If a cognition of the type of qualifier-and-qualificand is false, automatically the objects appearing in such a cognition lose their reality and consequently the relation presented in the cognition has to be treated as illusory and not real.

In this way once it is proved that a relation is false no reality of the external existence of the world can be established. Because if it is false it does not exist outside, if it does not exist outside it has no capacity to become a cause with reference to the production of a cognition and thereby the realists' slogan namely, *jñānādhīnā vastusattā* becomes empty.

Therefore, to me it appears that since Dharmakīrti wants to establish idealism of the type of Yogācāra Philosophy he has no other alternative left than to deny all relations on the basis of which the realists will explain a qualified cognition on the basis of which again, the reality of the word will be established by them. The assumption of the realists that a cognition is also produced by the external object cannot be accepted by the idealists.

Notes and References

1. *Siddhāntamuktāvalī*, Chowkhamba Edn, 1972, pp. 54-55.
2. *Viṣayanirūpyaṁ hi jñānam.*
3. The Mīmāṁsakas, though realists, do not accept inherence. In stead they accept a relation called *tādātmya* which is described as a relation such as identity-cum-difference (*bhedasahiṣṇu-abheda* or *bhedaghaṭita-abheda*). In any case, relation here is accepted as real one.
4. For instance, the knowledge the ground with the absence of a pot has *svarūpa sambandha* as its one of the objects because without the relation the absence of pot can not be called the qualifier of the ground.
5. *Pāratantryam hi sambandhaḥ*, *Sambandhaparīkṣā*, Verse No. 1, Dharmakīrtinibandhāvali, ed. by Dvarkanatha sastri, Bauddha-bharati, Varanasi, 1972. Hereafter referred to as SaPa.
6. *Rūpaśleṣo hi sambandhaḥ*, SaPa. 2.
7. *Parāpekṣā hi sambandhaḥ*, SaPa. 3.
8. *Kāryakāraṇabhāvo' pi (sambandhaḥ)*, SaPa. 7.
9. *Dviṣṭho hi kaścit sambandhaḥ*, SaPa. 11.
10. *Siddhe kā paratantratā, Sapa*. 1.
11. *Sambandhinor abhāve sambandhāyogāt*, Prabhācandra (Commentary on SaPa. printed together), p. 139.
12. *Rūpaśleṣo hi sambandho, dvitve sa ca katham bhavet*, SaPa. 2.
13. *Parāpekṣā hi sambandhaḥ, so 'san kaṭham apekṣate/samśva sarvaniāsaṁśo, bhāvaḥ katham apekṣate / /* SaPa. 3.
14. *Kāryakāranabhāvo' pi tagor asahabhāvataḥ prasiddhyati katham dviṣṭho' dviṣ the sambandhatā katham*, SaPa. 7.
15. *Sambandho naikavrttimān*, SaPa. 8.

16. *Yady apekṣya tayor ekam anyatrāsau pravartate upakārī hy apekṣyaḥ syāt katham copakaroty asau*, SaPa. 9.

17. *Yady ekārthābhisambandhāt kāryakāraṇatā tayoḥ prāptā dvitvābhisambandhāt* savyetaraviṣāṇayoḥ SaPa. 10.

18. *Tāv (=bhāvābhāvau) eva, kāraṇatatra kim*, SaPa. 12.

Here *bhāvābhāva* stands for what is known as *anvaya-vyatireka* i.e. *tat-sattve, tat-sattvam, tadabhāve tadabhāvaḥ*. Dharmakīrti wants to point out that the *anvaya-vyatireka* of x and y is nothing more than a condition and so there is nothing called a relation between x and y.

19. *Ayam śabdo niyoktāram samśritaḥ*, SaPa. 12.

20. *Bhinne kā ghaṭanā abhinne kāryakarṇatāpi kā*. SaPa. 18.

21. Bhāve hyanyasya viśliṣṭau śliṣṭau syātām katham ca tau, SaPa. 18.

22. *Saṁyogajanane' pīṣṭau tataḥ sāṁyoginau na tau/karmādiyogitā-patteḥ*, SaPa. 22.

23. SaPa. 22. simply contains *sthitiśca prativarṇitā* which is commented upon as *granthāntare pratikṣiptā, sthāphyasthāpakayoḥ janyajandkatvābhavāt nānya sthitir iti*, Prabhacandra, p. 149.

7.0 *CONCLUSION*

It can be observed that a Realist cannot portray the reality of this universe without accepting that the relations which appear in the qualified cognitions are as real as the relata. On the other hand, an idealist cannot afford to entertain any relation. Because acceptance of a relation amounts to acceptance of relata and if the very aim of an idealist is to deny the relata, the easiest way to achieve this goal is to deny the relation itself. Thus, acceptance of a relation amounts to acceptance of the relata and thereby, the acceptance of the reality of the relata i.e. of the world of ours. Similarly, the non-acceptance of a Relation amounts to non-acceptance of its Relata and thereby the non-acceptance of the reality of the world around us. This dichotomy can be generalised and extended to any philosophy which entertains that type of dichotomy of Realism and Idealism. Though it is very much daring and courageous on the part of Dharmakīrti to challenge the reality of the world around us, the main problem has remained unsolved whether the same argument can establish that an uncontradicted qualified cognition is erroneous. Unless that is established, and I think there is limitation imposed by Dharmakīrti himself on the authenticity of the form of argument itself, it cannot be held that he has succeeded in refuting all relations because unless it is accepted that the relations are true, the entire argument for refutation which involves relations cannot establish that the Relations are mental constructs and hence illusions Needless to say, the intension of Dharmakīrti in denying all relations is quite clear and I have simply tried to highlight it in this humble endeavour.

आचार्य धर्मकीर्तिविरचिता

सम्बन्धपरीक्षा

(प्रभाचन्द्रकृतव्याख्योपेता)

Sambandhaparīkṣā of Dharmakīrti

With the commentary of Prabhācandra

I

प्रभाचन्द्रटीका

ननु चाणूनामयः[1]शलाकाकल्पत्वेनान्योन्यं सम्बन्धाभावतः स्थूलादिप्रतीतेर्भ्रान्तत्वात् कथं तद्वशात् तत्स्वभावो भावः स्यात् ? तथा हि–सम्बन्धोऽर्थानां पारतन्त्र्यलक्षणो वा स्यात्, रूपश्लेषलक्षणो वा स्यात्, अनिष्पन्नयोर्वा ? न तावदनिष्पन्नयोः, स्वरूपस्यैवाऽसत्त्वात् शशाश्वविषाणवत् । निष्पन्नयोश्च पारतन्त्र्याभावादसम्बन्ध एव ।

उक्तञ्च—

सम्बन्ध परीक्षा

पारतन्त्र्यं हि सम्बन्धः सिद्धे[2] का परतन्त्रता[3] ।
तस्मात् सर्वस्य भावस्य सम्बन्धो नास्ति तत्त्वतः ।।१।।

---

१. रुपरसगन्धस्परर्शपरमाणूनां सजातीयविजातियव्यावृत्तानां परस्परमसम्बद्धानामित्यर्थः ।

२. सम्बन्धिनि ।

३. सह्यविन्ध्ययोरिव ।

I

(Prabhācandra=Prabhā Ca) :

Well, since the atoms are like iron-particles they are mutually unconnected and so the knowledge that something is a whole (made of parts) is nothing but an illusion, and in that case, how can a positive entity (*bhāvapadārtha*) be of the nature of a thing having a big size due to relation ? To put it precisely, the relation among the things can be either of the nature of dependency (*pāratantrya*) or of the nature of amalgamation of the forms of things (*rūpaśleṣa*); which one do you intend ? If you say the first one, (we ask you) whether this (=dependency) subsists between two already produced relata or 'between two relata' not (yet) produced ? You cannot maintain that it (=the dependency) is between two unproduced relata, because in that case it will loose its form itself (since there will be no relatum and so there can be no relation either) like the horns of hair and horse. And since there is no question of dependency when the things are already produced (independent of one another), one must accept that there is no relation at all.

And (this is what) is said (by Dharmakīrti in the following) :

Kārikā : *1*

(If someone says :) dependency, indeed, is the relation, (we ask him) where is the question of any dependency when (the relatum) is already established (i.e. already produced and existent). Therefore, in reality, there is no relation of (i.e. between) any positive entities.

(Prabhā Ca)

Nor can that (relation) be of the nature of amalgamation of the forms of thing, because if the relata are two distinct things then the amalgamation of forms is a contradictory idea. If both the relata are merged in one and the same thing then, verily, there is no relation at all because there can be no relation in the absence of two relata since a relation exists in two things (i.e. a relation requires two thing).

प्रभाचन्द्रटीका

नापि रूपश्लेषलक्षणोऽसौ,[४] सम्बन्धिनोरभावे सम्बन्धायोगात्, द्विष्ठत्वात्तस्य । अथ नैरन्तर्यं तयो रूपश्लेषः? न,[५] अस्यान्तरालाभावरूपत्वेनातात्त्विकत्वात् सम्बन्धरूपत्वायोगः । निरन्तरतायाश्च सम्बन्धरूपत्वे सान्तरतापि कथं सम्बन्धो न स्यात्[८] ?

---

४. अन्योन्यस्वभावानुप्रवेशलक्षणः ।

५. इति चेदित्युपरितः ।

६. अन्तरालाभावो नैरन्तर्यमिति ।

७. तुच्छभावरुपत्वादभावस्य ।

८. निरन्तरतावत्पदार्थद्वयापेक्षत्वाविशेषात् ।

(*Objection*) : Well, (if we say that) continuity or the state of having no gap between two things is the *rūpaśleṣa* of the two relata, then ?

(*Reply*) : No, Because it will become unreal since it (=*nairantarya*) means absence of gap (between the two relata) and so it will loose its character of being a relation (because it becomes a negative entity). Moreover, if the absence of gap is accepted as the relation why not the state of having gap or intervention be accepted as the relation ?

II

प्रभाचन्द्रटीका

किञ्च–असौ रूपश्लेषः सर्वात्मना, एकदेशेन वा स्यात् ? सर्वात्मना रूपश्लेषे अणूनां पिण्डः अणुमात्रः स्यात्। एकदेशेन तच्छ्लेषे किमेकदेशास्तस्यात्मभूताः,[९] परभूता वा ? आत्मभूताश्चेत्, न एकदेशेन रूपश्लेषस्तदभावात्[१०]। परभूताश्चेत्, तैरप्यणूनां सर्वात्मनैकदेशेन वा रूपश्लेषे स एव पर्यनुयोगः, अनवस्था च स्यात्। तदुक्तम्–

सम्बन्ध परीक्षा

रूपश्लेषो हि सम्बन्धो द्वित्वे[११] स च कथं भवेत्।
तस्मात्[१२] प्रकृतिभिन्नानां[१३] सम्बन्धो नास्ति तत्त्वतः ॥२॥

---

९. अंशाः।
१०. निरंशत्वादणोः।
११. सम्बन्धिनोः।
१२. प्रकृत्या=स्वभावेन।
१३. अणूनाम्।

II

(*Prabhā Ca*) :

Moreover, (we want to know) whether *rūpaśleṣa* (merging) means amalgamation with the entire thing or only with a part of that thing ? If you say that it is a total *rūpaśleṣa* (merging), then a bundle of the atoms will result (in reality) into a single atom only. If, on the other hand, you say that *rūpaśleṣa* occurs with a part (of the relata) then (we ask you) whether the parts (of the relata with which the *rūpaślṣa* is intended) are identical with the relata or different from the relata ? If you say that they are relata only, then there cannot be *rūpaśleṣa* with parts because there are no parts (since the atoms have no part). If (however, you say) that they (i.e. parts) are different from the relata then (again we ask you, whether these parts have total *rūpaśleṣa* with the atoms or with a part of them ? In any way, the same objection can be raised again (as raised above). Moreover, it will lead to endless regression. Therefore, (Dharmakīrti) says :—

Kārikā no. 2

(If you say that (*rūpaśleṣa*) (merging) or amalgamation can be the relation (between two things) then (we ask you) when the relata are two (which are required for calling something as a relation), then how is that (relation) possible because unless there are two relata there is no relation and if such a relation is a merging then there are no two relata and so, there is no relation). Therefore, the relata (positive entities) which are discrete by nature can have no relation, in fact.

III

प्रभाचन्द्रटीका

किञ्च—परापेक्षैव सम्बन्धः, तस्य द्विष्ठत्वात्। तं चापेक्षते भावः[१४] स्वयं सन्, असन् वा? न तावदसन्, अपेक्षाधर्माश्रयत्वविरोधात् खर-शृङ्गवत्। नापि सन्, सर्वनिराशंसत्वात्,[१५] अन्यथा[१६] सत्त्वविरोधात्। तन्न परापेक्षा नाम यद्रूपः सम्बन्धः सिद्धयेत्।

सम्बन्ध परीक्षा

उक्तञ्च—

परापेक्षा हि सम्बन्धः सोऽसन् कथमपेक्षते।[१७]
संश्च सर्वनिराशंसो भावः कथमपेक्षते ॥३॥

---

१४. सम्बन्धलक्षणः।

१५. सर्वेषु निराकाङ्क्षत्वात्।

१६. परमपेक्षते चेत्।

१७. परम्।

III

(Prabhā Ca) :

As a matter of fact, dependency on something else is, indeed, (the nature of) a relation, because it exists in two relata. A positive entity requires that (relation, this it what you say) : May I know whether the positive entity requires that being itself existent or being non-existent ? You cannot hold that the relata require it themselves being non-existent because a non-existent relatum cannot be the abode of the *apekṣādharma* (i.e. property of requiring something) like the horns of a hare. Nor can an existent positive *padārtha* (require that relation), because it has no expectancy whatsoever; otherwise (i e. if it is accepted that a positive entity has expectancy of other *padārtha* then) it will loose its character of being a discrete positive entity (also in that case a positive entity will have to exist more than one moment if it requires something else and so its character of being momentary will vanish and so it cannot be said to be a *sat-padārtha.* Because *sat-padārthas* are momentary only). Therefore, there is nothing called dependency and so a relation of that nature cannot be established.

So says (Dharmakīrti) :

Kārikā no. 3

If you say that dependency on something else is the relation then (we ask you) how can a non-existent *asat* require that ? And how can an existent positive entity (*sat-padārtha*) require that relation when by nature it is free from all dependency ?

IV

प्रभाचन्द्रटीका

किञ्च—असौ सम्बन्धः सम्बन्धिभ्यां भिन्नः, अभिन्नो वा ? यद्यभिन्नः, तदा सम्बन्धिनावेव, न सम्बन्धः कश्चित्, स एव वा, न ताविति ? भिन्नश्चेत्; सम्बन्धिनौ केवलौ[१७] कथं सम्बद्धौ स्याताम् ?

भवतु वा सम्बन्धोऽर्थान्तरम्;[१८] तथापि तेनैकेन सम्बन्धेन सह द्वयोः सम्बन्धिनोः कः सम्बन्ध ? यथा सम्बन्धिनोर्यथोक्तदोषान्न कश्चित् सम्बन्धः, तथात्रापि। तेनानयोः सम्बन्धान्तराभ्युपगमे चानवस्था स्यात्; तत्रापि सम्बन्धबुद्धिर्वास्तवी; तद्वयतिरेकेण अन्यस्य सम्बन्धस्यासम्भवात्। तदुक्तम्—

सम्बन्ध परीक्षा

द्वयोरेकाभिसम्बन्धात् सम्बन्धो यदि तद्द्वयोः[१९] ।
कः[२०] सम्बन्धोऽनवस्था[२१] च न सम्बन्धमतिस्तथा ।।४।।

---

१८. सम्बन्धरहितौ ।
१९. सम्बन्धिभ्याम् ।
२०. स च सम्बन्धिनौ च ।
२१. सम्बन्धसम्बन्धिनोः ।
२२. अन्यथेति शेषः ।

IV

(Prabhā Ca) :

Moreover, whether this relation (which you want to establish) is different from the two relata or identical with them ? If you say that it is identical (with them) then, (it amounts to saying that) there exist the two relata only, no relation (other than these relata) exists (there). Or, there exists mere relation and the two relata do not exist. If, on the other hand, you say that it is different (from the relata) then how can the two unconnected relata be connected.

Or, let the relation be a different entity from the two relata. Even then with that single relation what is the relation of the relata ?

As no relation can be accepted between the two relata because of the defects stated above in the above mentioned case (i.e. if the relation is identical with the relata then either there are only the relata or there is only the relation, so on and so forth), similarly, here also (there can be no relation possible). Therefore, if another relation is accepted between these two (i.e. the relation and the relatum) there will be endless regression, because there too another relation has to be accepted. Therefore, the knowledge that there is a relation between the two relata is not real, because there is nothing called relation there othere than the relata.

Therefore, (Dharmakīrti) says the following :

(*Kārikā no. 4*)

Since two relata are (realised as) connected with one thing, there is a relation, if (you say so, then we ask you) what is the relation between that relation and the relata ? (If you accept some other relation there) there will be endless regression. Thus, the knowledge of any relation there is not real one.

V

सम्बन्ध परीक्षा

ततः—

तौ च भावौ तदन्यश्च[२३] सर्वे ते स्वात्मनि स्थिताः ।
इत्यमिश्राः स्वयं भावास्तान् मिश्रयति कल्पना[२४] ॥५॥

प्रभाचन्द्रटीका

तौ च भावौ सम्बन्धिनौ ताभ्यामन्यश्च सम्बन्धः, सर्वे ते स्वात्मनि स्वस्वरूपे स्थिताः । तेनामिश्रा व्यावृत्तस्वरूपाः स्वयं भावाः, तथापि तान्मिश्रयति योजयति[२५] कल्पना ॥५॥

२३. सम्बन्धः ।
२४. वासनारुपा कर्त्री ।
२५. अवास्तवी ।

V

(Prabhā Ca):

(The following follows) from that :

Kārikā No. 5

(As a matter of fact) the two relata and (what you consider as) the additional entity called relation exist in their own forms. Therefore, (in reality) the positive entities, by themselves, are unrelated. It is the imagination (*vāsanā*) which mixes them (and so they appear as related).

(Prabhā Ca): The two are the relata and the relation is different from them; all these exist in their own forms. Therefore, the positive entities by themselves are unmixed discrete in nature. Still, the imagination (*vāsanā*) mixes, i.e. connects them.

VI

प्रभाचन्द्रटीका

अत[२६] एव तद्वास्तवसम्बन्धाभावेऽपि तामेव कल्पनामनुरुन्धानैर्व्यवहर्तृभिर्भावानां[२७] भेदोऽन्यापोहः,[२८] तस्य प्रत्यायनाय क्रियाकारकादिवाचिनः शब्दाः प्रयोज्यन्ते—'देवदत्त गामभ्याज शुक्लां दण्डेन' इत्यादयः। न खलु कारकाणां क्रियया सम्बन्धोऽस्ति; क्षणिकत्वेन क्रियाकाले कारकाणामसम्भवात्। उक्तञ्च—

सम्बन्ध परीक्षा

तामेव[२९] चानुरुन्धानैः क्रियाकारकवाचिनः ।
भावभेदप्रतीत्यर्थं संयोज्यन्तेऽभिधायकाः ॥६॥

---

२६. कल्पनैव मिश्रयति यतः ।

२७. स्थिरस्थूलसाधारणाकाररूपः ।

२८. अगोव्यावृत्तिर्गौः, अघटव्यावृत्तिर्घट इत्यादि ।

२९. कल्पनामवास्तवीं बुद्धिम् ।

VI

(Prabhā Ca) ;

This is the reason why following this imagination (*vāsanā*), in spite of the absence of any real relation between the two relata the speakers use the words expressive of action, *kāraka*, etc. namely, 'Devadatta drove the white cow with the stick' and the like in order to convey the (mutual) difference i.e. the difference of one positive entity from the rest. (In fact,) there is no relation of any *kāraka* factor or accomplisher with the action, because it is impossible for any *kāraka* (accomplisher) to exist at the time of action since everything is momentary. It is corroborated (by Dharmakīrti) as follows :—

Kārikā No. 6

Following the same (imagination) *vāsanā*, people construct words expressive of an action and a *kāraka* in order to convey the difference of the positive entity.

VII

सम्बन्ध परीक्षा

कार्यकारणभावोपि[३०] तयोरसहभावतः ।
प्रसिद्धयति कथं द्विष्ठोऽद्विष्ठे सम्बन्धता कथम् ।।७।।

प्रभाचन्द्रटीका

कार्यकारणभावस्तर्हि सम्बन्धो भविष्यति— इत्यप्यसमीचीनम्, कार्यकारणयोरसहभावतस्तस्यापि[३१] द्विष्ठस्यासम्भवात् । न खलु कारणकाले कार्यं तत्काले वा कारणमस्ति, तुल्यकालं कार्यकारणभावानुपपत्तेः, सव्येतरगोविषाणवत् । तन्न सम्बन्धिनौ[३२] सहभाविनौ विद्यते येनानयोर्वर्त्तमानोऽसौ सम्बन्धः स्यात् । अद्विष्ठे च[३३] भावे सम्बन्धतानुपपन्नैव ।।७।।

---

३०. सामान्यसम्बन्धं सन्दूष्य सम्बन्धविशेषं दूषयन्नाह ।

३१. क्षणिकत्वात् ।

३२. कार्यकारणलक्षणौ ।

३३. कार्यकारणलक्षणे ।

VII

Kārikā No. 7

(Similarly), how can even the cause and effect relationship (existing in two things) be possible, because the cause and the effect do not co-exist ? If it cannot exist in two how can it be called a relation ?

(Prabhā Ca) :

(*Objection*) :—Then, let the cause—and—effect relationship be a relation.

(Reply) Even this is not proper. Because the cause and the effect do not exist together and so even this (cause-and-effect relationship) cannot be possible, since it does not exist in two. It is not the fact that at the time of cause there is effect or at the time of effect there is cause, because if they are at the same time it is impossible to say that one is the cause and the other is the effect as in the case of the left and the right horns of the cow (existing at one time). Therefore, the two relata do not exist together at one time. Had it been so, one could have said there is a relation existent between the two relata. And when the relation such as the cause-and-effect relationship does not exist in two, naturally it cannot be taken as a relation.

VIII

सम्बन्ध परीक्षा

क्रमेण भाव एकत्र[३४] वर्तमानोऽन्यनिस्पृहः ।
तदभावेऽपि[३५] तद्भावात्[३६] सम्बन्धो नैकवृत्तिमान् ॥८॥

प्रभाचन्द्रटीका

कार्ये कारणे वा क्रमेणासौ सम्बन्धो वर्तते—इत्यप्यसाम्प्रतम्; यतः क्रमेणापि भावः सम्बन्धाख्य एकत्र कारणे कार्ये वा वर्त्तमानोऽन्यनिस्पृहः = कार्यकारणयोरन्यतरानपेक्षो[३७] नैकवृत्तिमान् सम्बन्धो युक्तः, तदभावेपि = कार्य[३८] कारणयोरभावेऽपि[३९] तद्भावात् ॥८॥

---

३४. कार्ये कारणे वा ।
३५. तयोः कार्यकारणयोः ।
३६. तस्य = सम्बन्धस्य ।
३७. 'अन्यनिस्पृहस्य' प्रत्यर्थः ।
३८. प्रत्यर्थः ।
३९. अन्यतरस्य ।

VIII

Kārikā No. 8

The cause-and-effect relationship, although exists in one of the relata by succession still, does not require another relatum (for its existence) and since in spite of the absence of one relatum it can exist in another the relation which exists in only one thing cannot be taken as a relation.

(Prabhā Ca) :

If you say that the cause-and-effect relationship exists, in succession, either in the effect or in the cause, it is also improper. Because the positive entity, namely, the relation, even if, exists in one i.e either in the cause or in the effect, it remains independent i.e. not depending either on the cause or on the effect. It is not proper to take a thing as relation if it exists in only one thing, **because even in the absence of either the cause or the effect it can exist.**

IX

सम्बन्ध परीक्षा

यद्यपेक्ष्य तयोरेकमन्यत्रासौ प्रवर्तते ।
उपकारी ह्यपेक्ष्यः स्यात् कथं चोपकरोत्यसन् ॥९॥

प्रभाचन्द्रटीका

यदि पुनः कार्यकारणयोरेकं कार्यं कारणं[४०] वापेक्ष्यान्यत्र कार्ये कारणे वासौ सम्बन्धः क्रमेण वर्त्तत इति[४१] सस्पृहत्वेन द्विष्ठ एवेष्यते; तदानेनापेक्ष्यमाणेनोपकारिणा[४३] भवितव्यम्, यस्मादुपकार्यपेक्ष्यः स्यात्,[४४] नान्यः। कथं चोपकरोत्यसन्? यदा कारणकाले कार्याख्यो भावोऽसन् तत्काले वा कारणाख्यस्तदा नैवोपकुर्याद्;[४५] असामर्थ्यात्[४६] ॥९॥

---

४०. अस्य कार्यस्येदं कारणमिति ।
४१. हेतोः ।
४२. कार्येण कारणेन वा ।
४३. सम्बन्धेन ।
४४. लोके ।
४५. कार्यं कारणमपेक्ष्य कारणे कार्यमपेक्ष्य यो वर्त्तते सम्बन्धस्तम् ।
४६. खरविषाणादिवत् ।

IX

Kārikā No. 9

(If it is said that) the cause-and-effect relationship operates requiring one of the two with regard to the other (i.e. with reference to either the cause or the effect), (it will not be proper to say so) because that which is required for something helps i.e. brings about some effect to that thing, but how can an entity bring about some effect without being present there ?

(Prabhā Ca) :

If however, (you say that) the cause-and-effect relationship exists in succession either in the cause or in the effect with reference to some effect or cause and so since one requires the other, this relation of cause-and-effect (is intended as) remaining in two things and thus it can be taken as a relation, then this is what is required by the other must be regarded as bringing about some effect to the other. Because that which brings about some effect is alone required and not anything else. But how can an entity help without existing at that time ? When at the time of the cause, the effect is not present or at the time of effect there is no cause present, neither of the two can bring about any effect in the other, because they do not have the capacity to do so.

X

सम्बन्ध परीक्षा

यद्येकार्थाभिसम्बन्धात् कार्यकारणता तयोः ।
प्राप्ता द्वित्वादिसम्बन्धात् सव्येतरविषाणयोः ॥१०॥

प्रभाचन्द्रटीका

किञ्च—यद्येकार्थाभिसम्बन्धात्[४७] कार्यकारणता तयोः कार्यकारणभावत्वेनाभिमतयोः; तर्हि द्वित्वसंख्या[४८]परत्वापरत्वविभागादिसम्बन्धात्[४९] प्राप्ता सा सव्येतरगोविषाणयोरपि[५०] ॥१०॥

---

४७. सम्बन्धलक्षण ।

४८. द्वन्द्वः ।

४९. आदिना पृथक्त्वादि ।

५०. द्वित्वसंख्यालक्षणैकार्थाभिसम्बन्धस्याविशेषात् ।

X

Kārikā No. 10

If (it is argued that) two things can have the cause-and-effect relationship provided they are related to one thing (namely, the relation) then there will arise the contingency of the left and right horns (of a cow) becoming mutually cause and effect to each other because, both of them are connected with the number two etc.

(Prabhā Ca) :

Moreover, if it is accepted that there can be cause-and-effect relationship between a cause and its effect because of their being connected with one thing (namely, the relation), then there will arise the contingency of thc left horn of a cow becoming the cause of the right or *vice versa* because these two horns are also connected with number two, farness, nearness, separation, etc.

XI

सम्बन्ध परीक्षा

द्विष्ठो हि कश्चित् सम्बन्धो नातोऽन्यत्तस्य लक्षमण ।

प्रभाचन्द्रटीका

न येन केनचिदेकेन सम्बन्धात् सेष्यते; किं तर्हि ? सम्बन्धलक्षणेनैवेति[५१] चेत्; तन्न, द्विष्ठो हि कश्चित्पदार्थः सम्बन्धः, नातोऽर्थद्वयाभिसम्बन्धादन्यत् तस्य लक्षणम् येनास्य संख्यादेर्विशेषो व्यवस्थाप्यैत ॥११॥

५१. एकेन सह ।

XI

Kārikā No. 11

A relation is that which exists in two things. There is no other definition (of relation) other than this.

(Prabhā Ca) :

(Objection) :— We do not say that if two things are connected with any one thing there is cause-and-effect relationship.

(Reply) : Then what (do you say) ?

(Objection) : (We say) only when two things are connected by a relation as defined' (i.e. that which exists in two things), that relation is called the cause-and-effect relation.

(Reply) : This is not correct. Because somethīng is called a relation if it exists in two things. There is no other definition of relation other than this. Had there been some other definition possible, one could have distinguished number etc. from that relation.

XII

सम्बन्ध परीक्षा

भावाभावोपधिर्योगः[५२] कार्यकारणता यदि ॥११॥

योगोपाधी न तावेव कार्यकारणतात्र किम् ।

भेदाच्चेन्नन्वयं शब्दो नियोक्तारं[५३] समाश्रितः ॥१२॥

प्रभाचन्द्रटीका

कस्यचिद्भावे[५४] भावोऽभावे[५५] चाभावः[५६], तावुपाधि विशेषणं यस्य योगस्य = सम्बन्धस्य स कार्यकारणता यदि न सर्वसम्बन्धः, तदा तावेव योगोपाधी[५७] भावाभावौ कार्यकारणतास्तु[५८], किमसत्सम्बन्धकल्पनया ? भेदाच्चेत्[५९] 'भावे हि भावोऽभावे[६०] चाभावः' इति[६१] बह्वोऽभिधेयाः[६२] कथं कार्यकारणतेत्येकार्थाभिधायिना शब्देनोच्यन्ते ? नन्वयं शब्दो[६३] नियोक्तारं समाश्रितः। नियोक्ता हि यं शब्दं यथा[६४] प्रयुङ्क्ते तथा प्राह[६५], इत्यनेकत्राप्येका[६६] श्रुतिर्न विरुध्यते इति तावेव कार्यकारणता ॥१२॥

---

५२. सम्बन्धः ।

५३. नरम् ।

५४. कार्यस्य कारणस्य वा ।

५५. कार्यकारणतायाः स्यात् ।

५६. भावाभावौ ।

५७. उपाधिः = विशेषणम् ।

५८. सम्बन्धः ।

५९. जैनानाशङ्क्याह बौद्धः ।

६०. भावाभावाभ्यां कार्यकारणभावसम्बन्धस्य ।

६१. सम्बन्धस्य ।

६२. चत्वारोऽर्थाः ।

६३. कार्यकारणसम्बन्धप्रतिपादकः कार्यकारणलक्षणः ।

६४. एकार्थमभिप्रेत्यानेकार्थं वाभिप्रेत्य ।

६५. एकार्थानेकार्थान् वा ।

६६. यथोदधिशब्दः उदकानि अस्मिन्धीयन्ते स उदधिरित्यादिः ।

XII

Kārikā No. 11-12

If (you say that) cause-and-effect relationship is the relation which is of the nature of *anvaya-vyatireka* (i.e. in the presence of a cause an effect is seen and in the absence of it no effect is seen), then why not the same two (*bhāvābhāva* i.e. *anvayavyatireka*) be taken as the cause-and-effect relationship ? If you say that they are different, then this word (one will have to say) depends on the speaker.

(Prabhā Ca) :

In the presence of something, something comes into existence and in the absence of that it does not come into existence; whose qualifiers are these two aspects that is called the cause-and-effect relationship and not any relation whatsoever. If this is so, then let those very two aspects (*bhāvābhāva*) be taken as the cause-and-effect relatinship; what is the need of postulating an unreal relation ?

If you say that *anvayavyatireka* is different from cause-and-effect then how is it that the word *kāryakāraṇatā* expresses many things such as "in presence of something, something comes into existence and in the absence of it, it does not come into being" ?

Well, the usage of a word depends on the speaker. A word expresses that sense in which sense the speaker uses it and so there is no difficulty even though a single word (*Kāraṇatā*) stands for many senses. Therefore, those very two aspects (*anvayavyatireka*) can be (your *kārya-kāraṇatā*, and there is no independent relation called *kāryakāraṇatā* as such).

XIII

सम्बन्ध परीक्षा

पश्यन्नेकम[६७] दृष्टस्य[६८] दर्शने तददर्शने ।[६९]
अपश्यनकार्यमन्वेति विना व्याख्यातृभिर्जनः ॥१३॥

प्रभाचन्द्रटीका

यस्मात् पश्यन्नेकं कारणाभिमतमुपलब्धिलक्षणप्राप्तस्याऽदृष्टस्य[७०] कार्याख्यस्य दर्शने सति तददर्शने च सत्यपश्यन्कार्यमन्वेति[७१] 'इदमतो भवति' इति[७२] प्रतिपद्यते जनः 'अत इदं जातम'[७३] इत्याख्यातृभिर्विनापि ॥१३॥

---

६७. कारणम् ।

६८. कार्यस्य ।

६९. तस्य = कारणस्य ।

७०. कारणाभिमतपदार्थदर्शनात् पूर्वम् ।

७१. कथम् तथा हि ।

७२. स्वयम् ।

७३. शब्दोल्लेखमन्तरेण उपदेशकः पुरूषैः ।

XIII

Kārikā No. 13

Observing one (i.e. the cause) when a person comes to know that (i.e. the effect) which was not seen (at the time of seeing the cause) and when he does not find the effect in the absence of that cause, even without the help of an interpreter he relates the effect to that cause (i.e. he comes to know that this is the effect of that cause i.e. he finds cause-and-effect relationship between the two).

(Prabhā Ca) :

Since after seeing one thing which is intended as the cause if the unseen effect which can be verified by the knowledge is seen, and since when one does not see the cause and thereby he does not see the effect, he, then, connects that "This comes from this", This is produced from this" etc. without the help of any interpreter.

XIV

सम्बन्ध परीक्षा

दर्शनादर्शने मुक्त्वा कार्यबुद्धेरसम्भवात् ।
कार्यादिश्रुतिरप्यत्र लाघवार्थं निवेशिता ॥१४॥

प्रभाचन्द्रटीका

तस्माद[७४] दर्शनादर्शने[७५] विषयिणि[७६] विषयोपचारात्—भावाभावौ मुक्त्वा कार्यबुद्धेरसम्भवात्[७७] कार्यादिश्रुतिरप्यत्र[७८] भावाभावयोर्मा लोकः[७९] प्रतिपदमियतीं[८०] शब्दमालामभिदध्यात्' इति व्यवहारलाघवार्थं[८१] निवेशितेति[८२] ॥१४॥

---

७४. कारणस्य ।

७५. कार्यस्य ।

७६. कार्यकारणताभिमतयोः पदार्थयोः कार्यकारणता भवत्विति ।

७७. दर्शनादर्शनलक्षणे ज्ञाने ।

७८. भावाभावावेव कार्यं, नान्यदित्यर्थः ।

७९. श्रुतिः = शब्दः ।

८०. न केवलं कार्यकारणश्रुतिः, किन्तु ।

८१. भावे भावः, अभावे चाऽभावः इत्येतावतीम् ।

८२. समर्थिता ।

XIV

Kārikā No. 14

Since it is impossible to have the knowledge of effect without seeing and not seeing (of the cause) the word *kārya* etc. also is used here for the sake of simplicity.

(Prabhā Ca) :

Therefore, in the seeing and not seeing (of the cause) there is seeing and not-seeing of the effect and so in the knowledge the object is superimposed and therefore without the *bhāva* and *abhāva* i.e. *anvaya* and *vyatireka*, no knowledge of effect can be possible. Therefore, the word *kārya* etc. is used here in order to simplify the usage so that people may not use many words in each case for *bhāva* and *abhāva*.

XV

सम्बन्ध परीक्षा

तद्भावाभावात्[७४] तत्कार्यगतिर्याप्यनुवर्ण्यते।[७५]
सङ्केतविषयाख्या सा सास्नादेर्गोगतिर्यथा[७६] ॥१५॥

प्रभाचन्द्रटीका

अन्वयव्यतिरेकाभ्यां[७७] कार्यकारणता नान्या चेत् कथं भावाभावाभ्यां सा प्रसाध्यते[७८] ? तदभावाभावात्[७९] लिङ्गात् तत्कार्यतागतिर्याप्यनुवर्ण्यते[८०]—अस्येदं कार्यं कारणं च' इति, सङ्केतविषयाख्या सा। यथा 'गौरयं सास्नादिमत्वात्[८१]' इत्यनेन गोव्यवहारस्य विषयः प्रदर्श्यते ॥१५॥

---

७४. तस्य=कारणस्य।

७५. तस्य=कारणस्य।

७६. साधनात्।

७७. भावाभावाभ्यामनुमीयमाना यदि कार्यकारणता ताभ्याम् अन्या तदा दूषणम्।

७८ सम्बन्धवादिना।

७९. तस्य=कारणस्य।

८०. अस्य कारणस्येदं कार्यम्, अस्य च कार्यस्येदं कारणमिति।

८१. अनुमानेन।

XV

Kārikā No. 15

You have explained that in the presence and absence of cause one gets the knowledge of (presence and absence of) effect. This is nothing but the object of *saṅketa* (for usage) as cow is understood on the basis of (the *saṅketa* of) *sāsnā* etc.

(Prabhā Ca):

If cause-and-effect relationship is not different from the positive and negative reasoning then how can that be established by presence and absence ?

You have explained that on the basis of the presence and absence of the cause one gets the knowledge of (the presence and absence of) the effect, e.g. "This is the effect of it and this is the cause of it". This is nothing but the object of communicational sign (*saṅketa*), as such a relationship is established by the statement "this is cow, because it has *sāsnā* etc". This refers to the object of the verbal usage 'go'.

XVI

सम्बन्ध परीक्षा

भावे भाविनि तद्भावो भाव एव च भाविता ।[82]
प्रसिद्धे हेतुफलते प्रत्यक्षानुपलम्भतः[83] ॥१६॥

प्रभाचन्द्रटीका

यतश्च[84] 'भावे[85] भाविनि=भवनधर्मिणि तद्भावः=कारणाभिमतस्य भाव एव कारणत्वम्. भावे एव कारणाभिमतस्य भाविता कार्याभिमतस्य कार्यत्वम्' इति प्रसिद्धे प्रत्यक्षानुपलम्भतो हेतु फलते। ततो भावाभावावेव कार्यकारणता, नान्या ॥१६॥

८२. कार्यता ।

८३. अन्वयव्यतिरेकतः ।

८४. प्रकारान्तरेण तावेव कार्यकारणतेति निरूपयति ।

८५. कार्यलक्षणे ।

XVI

Kārikā No. 16

When an effect comes into existence, there is existence of that (what is intended as cause) and when the effect comes into existence then alone there is effectness (in that). (So) the cause and effect relationship is well known from the presence and absence.

(Prabhā Ca) :

And because after the existence of an effect produced there is existence of cause i e. when there is effect then alone the question of causality comes. In the existence of effect alone that which is intended as cause gets the character of effectness. So from the knowledge of presence and absence one comes to know what the cause is and what the effect is. Therefore, the cause-and-effect relationship is nothing more than presence and absence (of what is intended as cause-and-effect).

XVII

सम्बन्ध परीक्षा

एतावन्मात्रतत्त्वार्थाः कार्यकारणगोचराः ।
विकल्पा दर्शयन्त्यर्थान् मिथ्यार्था घटितानिव ।।१७।।

प्रभाचन्द्रटीका

तेनैतावन्मात्रं=भावाभावौ तावेव[८६] तत्त्वं[८७] यस्यार्थस्यासावेतावन्मात्र-तत्त्वः, सोऽर्थो[८८] येषां[८९] विकल्पानां ते एतावन्मात्रतत्त्वार्थाः=एतावन्मात्र-बीजाः कार्यकारणगोचराः, दर्शयन्ति[९०] घटितानिव–सम्बद्धानिवास-म्बद्धानप्यर्थान् । एवं घटनाच्च मिथ्यार्थाः[९१] ।।१७।।

---

८६. स्वरूपम् ।

८७. कार्यकारणस्य ।

८८. अर्थः=विषयः ।

८९. भ्रान्तज्ञानानाम् ।

९०. विकल्पाः ।

९१. विकल्पाः ।

XVII

Kārikā No. 17

It is the imaginations, which correspond to merely this much fact i.e. mere *anvaya* and *vyatireka*, and which present two things as cause and effect, and which show the things as if they are related (but in reality they are not related) and hence the imaginations are false.

(Prabhā Ca) :

Therefore, *etāvanmātram* means mere *anvaya* and the *vyatireka* and *etāvanmātratattva* means 'whose reality boils down to only those two (*anvaya* and *vyatireka*)'; and *etāvanmātratattvārthāḥ* means 'whose i.e. of the *vikalpas* that (*etāvvnmātratattva*)is the meaning' i.e., which have these two alone as the basis, known as cause and effect; (the *vikalpas*) show (things) as *ghaṭita* i.e. as connected or related although they are, in fact, not related. And since they (*vikalpas*) show things as connected in spite of their not being connected in reality, they are false.

XVIII

सम्बन्ध परीक्षा

**भिन्ने का[९२] घटनाऽभिन्ने कार्यकारणतापि का ।
भावे ह्यन्यस्य[९३] विश्लिष्टौ श्लिष्टौ स्यातां कथं च तौ ॥१८॥**

प्रभाचन्द्रटीका

किञ्च, असौ कार्यकारणभूतोऽर्थो भिन्नः[९४], अभिन्नो वा स्यात्? यदि भिन्नः; तर्हि भिन्ने का घटना[९५] स्वस्वभावव्यवस्थितेः[९६] ? अथाभिन्नः; तदाऽभिन्ने कार्यकारणतापि का ? नैव स्यात् ।

स्यादेतत् न भिन्नस्याभिन्नस्य[९७] वा सम्बन्धः । किं तर्हि ? सम्बन्धाख्येनैकेन सम्बन्धात्; इत्यत्रापि भावे[९८] सत्तायामन्यस्य[९९] सम्बन्धस्य विश्लिष्टौ[१००] कार्यकारणाभिमतौ श्लिष्टौ स्याताम् ।

---

९२. सम्बन्धः ।

९३. सम्बन्धस्य ।

९४. परस्परम् ।

९५. सम्बन्धः ।

९६. कार्यकारणयोः ।

९७. कार्यस्य कारणस्य वा ।

९८. प्रत्यर्थोऽयम् ।

९९. भिन्नस्य ।

१००. स्वरूपेण ।

XVIII

Kārikā No. 18

When two things are different where is the question of any relation between them ? And if they are not different where is the question of any cause-and-effect relationship also ? If there is another relation between them the two separate things could come together. But how could they ?

(Prabhā Ca) :

Moreover, (may we ask you) whether the things intended as cause and effect are different or identical ? If you say that they are different, how can there be any relation between two different things because they are existent in their own form ?

If you say that they are identical then what sort of cause-and-effect relationship is possible there ? It is impossible indeed.

It can be put as follows.

It is not the case that something is a relation between two different or two identical things. Then what ? (What we say is this that something is called relation) because (two things) are related with that one thing called relation. Here too, had a separate relation existed (between the relation and the relatum), two separate things intended as cause and effect would have come together.

XIX

सम्बन्ध परीक्षा

संयोगिसमवाय्यादि सर्वमेतेन चिन्तितम् ।
अन्योन्यानुपकाराच्च न सम्बन्धी च तादृशः ॥१९॥

प्रभाचन्द्रटीका

कथ च तौ संयोगिसमवायिनौ ? आदिग्रहणात्[१०१] स्वस्वाम्यादिकम्[१०२] । सर्वमेतेनानन्तरोक्तेन सामान्यसम्बन्धप्रतिषेधेन चिन्तितम्[१०३] संयोग्यादीनामन्योन्यमनुपकाराच्चाजन्यजनकभावाच्च न सम्बस्धी[१०४] च तादृशोऽनुपकार्योपकारकभूतः ॥११॥

---

१०१. कारिकायाम् ।

१०२. स्वामिभृत्यभावसम्बन्धादिकम् ।

१०३. निराकृतम् ।

१०४. अर्थः ।

XIX

Kārikā No. 19

By this (negation of relation in general, the question of relation in) all connected, inherent etc. are taken into consideration and examined. Since there cannot be mutual help to bring about any effect (between) the two relata because they are momentary) there cannot be any such relatum).

(Prabhā Ca) :

And what about those which are connected and inherent ? By the mention of the word *ādi* (in the verse) one can include owner—and owned relation and the like.

All this has been taken into consideration by this aforesaid negation of relation in general (and the existence of any relation is refuted). And since there can be no mutual help to bring about any effect between (the two relata namely), the connected and the inherent and since there can be no cause-and-effect relation there, there is no object which can be of the nature of being helper of something.

XX

सम्बन्ध परीक्षा

जननेऽपि हि कार्यस्य केनचित् समवायिना ।
समवायी तदा नासौ न ततोऽतिप्रसङ्गतः ॥२०॥

प्रभाचन्द्रटीका

अथास्ति कश्चित्[१०५] समवायी[१०६] योऽवयविरूपं कार्यं जनयति, अतो नानुपकारापकारादसम्बन्धितेति; तन्न; यतो जननेऽपि कार्यस्य केनचित् समवायिनाभ्युपगम्यमाने[१०७] समवायी[१०८], नासौ तदा; जननकाले कार्यस्यानिष्पत्तेः ।[१०९] न च ततो जननात् समवायित्वं[११०] सिद्धयति; कुम्भकारादेरपि घटे समवायित्वप्रसङ्गात् ॥२०॥

---

१०५. उपकारकः ।

१०६. तन्त्वादिना ।

१०७. सम्बन्धवादिःन ।

१०८. कार्येण समम् ।

१०९. समवायिना कारणेन कार्यस्य निष्पादनसमये कार्यस्यानिष्पन्नत्वात् कुतः कार्येण समत्वं कारणस्य ? तत्करणे सति तस्य विनष्टत्वात् ।

११०. तन्तूनाम् ।

XX

Kārikā No. 20

Even if some material cause produces some effect, at the time of production of the effect that intended as material cause does not remain as material cause (because the effect is not yet produced). One cannot say that (it can be material cause) after the production of the effect, because in that case there will be over-extension (of the concept of Samavāyi-Kāraṇa).

(Prabhā Ca) :

(Objection) : Well, there is some material cause which produces the effect i.e. the whole. Therefore, it cannot be said that it does not bring about anything to the effect and so there can be no (cause-and-effect) relationship.

(Reply) : It is not true. Because for the production of an effect, even if, some material cause is accepted, at that time, it cannot be called material cause because at the time of production of the effect the effect is not yet accomplished. One cannot argue that since the accomplishment of the effect arises from that (cause), that can be treated as material cause, because in that case the potter etc. will have also to be accepted as material cause of pot.

XXI

सम्बन्ध परीक्षा

तयोरनुपकारेऽपि[111] समवाये परत्र वा ।
सम्बन्धो यदि[112] विश्वं स्यात् समवायि परस्परम् ।।२१।।

प्रभाचन्द्रटीका

तयोः[113] समवायिनोः परस्परमनुपकारेऽपि ताभ्यां वा समवायस्य नित्यतया समवायेन वा तयोः परत्र[114] वा क्वचिदनुपकारेऽपि सम्बन्धो यदीष्यते; तदा विश्वं परस्परासम्बद्धं समवायि परस्परं स्यात्[115] ।।२१।।

१११. समवायिनोः ।
११२. तर्हीति शेषः ।
११३. तन्तुपटयोः ।
११४. असमवायिनि कारणे कार्ये वा ।
११५. उपकारकत्वाभावविशेषात् ।

XXI

Kārikā No. 21

In spite of the fact that two things related with inherence do not bring about any effect in each other and still if you want to accept a relation either in the material cause or in the inherence, then each and everything in this universe will be mutually with inherence.

(Prabhā Ca) :

Although there is no mutual effect between two things related with inherence and in spite of the fact that neither these two help the inherence, nor the inherence helps these two still if you want to accept a relation, then all things, mutually unconnected, will have to be accepted as mutually connected with inherence (because bringing about some effect is not requierd by you).

XXII

सम्बन्ध परीक्षा

संयोगजननेऽपीष्टौ ततः संयोगिनौ न तौ ।[११६]
कर्मादियोगितापत्तेः स्थितिश्च प्रतिवर्णिता ॥२२॥

प्रभाचन्द्रटीका

इत्याचार्यधर्मकीर्तिविरचिता सम्बन्ध परीक्षा समाप्ता ।

यदि च संयोगस्य[११७] कार्यत्वात् तस्य ताभ्यां[११८] जननात् संयोगिता तयोः[११९] तदा संयोगजननेऽपीष्टौ, ततः संयोगजननान्न तौ संयोगिनौ, कर्मणोऽपि[१२०] संयोगिता[१२१]पत्तेः[१२२]। संयोगो ह्यन्यतरकर्मजः[१२३] उभयकर्मजश्चेष्यते[१२४]। आदिग्रहणात्[१२५] संयोगस्यापि[१२६] संयोगिता स्यात्[१२७]। न संयोगजननात् संयोगिता किन्तर्हि ? स्थापनादिति[१२८] चेत्; न स्थितिश्च[१२९] प्रतिवर्णिता[१३०] =ग्रन्थान्तरे प्रतिक्षिप्ता[१३१] स्थाप्यस्थापकयोर्जन्यजनकत्वाभावान्नान्या स्थितिरिति[१३२] ॥२२॥

इति प्रभाचन्द्रकृता सम्बन्धपरीक्षाव्याख्या समाप्ता[१३३] ॥

---

११६. कुतः ? यतः ।

११७. सम्बन्धस्य ।

११८. समवायिभ्याम् ।

११९. संयोगिनोः ।

१२०. क्रियायाः ।

१२१. कर्मणः सकाशात्संयोगजननात् ।

१२२. तथा च द्रव्ययोरेव हि संयोगः न कर्मणोरेवेति मतं विघटेत ।

१२३. शैलश्येनयोः ।

१२४. मल्लयोः ।

१२५. कारिकायाम् ।

१२६. गुणरूपस्य ।

१२७. हस्तपुस्तकसंयोगात्कायपुस्तकसंयोगस्योत्पत्तेः ।

१२८. संयोगिभ्यां स्थाप्यपदार्थस्य संयोगलक्षणस्य स्थितिनिष्पादनात् ।

१२९. संयोगिनोः संयोगस्य च ।

१३०. निराकृता ।

१३१. प्रत्यर्थः ।

१३२. जन्यजनकभावस्तु प्राक् प्रतिक्षिप्त इत्यर्थः ।

१३३. इतोऽग्रे भोटभाषानुवादे अन्या अपि तिस्रः कारिकाः समुपलभ्यन्ते, परन्तु तासां संस्कृतमूलं नोपलब्धमिति अत्र नैवोद्धृताः । जिज्ञासुभिस्तु तास्तत एवावगन्तव्याः ॥

XXII

Kārikā No. 22

(If you say that) the contact is produced (by the two connected things) then (we say that) those two things cannot be called connected simply because they produce contact, because in that case the action (which produces the contact) has also to be accepted as conneeted (because action also produces contact). (If you say that since the two things coming together bring into existence the contact and so they are *saṁyogins* then this argument of) existence is also refuted (else where).

(Prabhā Ca) :

If (it is ergued that) since 'contact' is a product and since it is produced by two things these two aae called connected then (one has to understand that) since they produce cantact, they are called connected. In that case (we say that) since 'contact' is produced by them they are not connected ones because (if that is accepted then) action will also have to be accepted as connected. Contact is (sometimes) produced by the action of either of the things to be connected or by the action of both the things to be connected. By the mention of the word ādi (in the verse 22) it is implied that even the contact will be called eonnected.

(Objector) : (we do not say that) since two things produce contact therefore, they are connected.

(Buddh.) Then what ?

(Objector) : Because these two bring into existence (the contact) therefore, they are called connected.

(Reply) : It is not true. (The argument of) existence (of contact) is refuted i.e. refuted in other works.

Since there is no cause-and.effect relationship between the *sthāpya* (i.e.) the contact) and the *sthāpaka* (i.e. the things to be connected) there is no other existence (of contact).

[Here ends the commentary on *Sambandhaparīksīā* (of Dharmakirti) by Prabhācandra.

Index

अनुक्रमणिकाः